# The Dancing God

*The Dancing God: Staging Hindu Dance in Australia* charts the sensational and historic journey of de-provincialising and popularising Hindu dance in Australia.

In the late nineteenth and early twentieth centuries, colonialism, orientalism and nationalism came together in various combinations to make traditional Hindu temple dance into a global art form. The intricately symbolic Hindu dance in its vital form was virtually unseen and unknown in Australia until an Australian impresario, Louise Lightfoot, brought it onto the stage. Her experimental changes, which modernised Kathakali dance through her pioneering collaboration with Indian dancer Ananda Shivaram, moved the Hindu dance from the sphere of ritualistic practice to formalised stage art. Amit Sarwal argues that this movement enabled both the authentic Hindu dance and dancer to gain recognition worldwide and created in his persona a cultural guru and ambassador on the global stage.

Ideal for anyone with an interest in global dance, *The Dancing God* is an in-depth study of how a unique dance form evolved in the meeting of travellers and cultures.

**Dr. Amit Sarwal** is a senior lecturer in literature at the University of the South Pacific, an affiliate member of the Contemporary Histories Research Group at Deakin University and the founding convenor of the Australia-India Interdisciplinary Research Network. His areas of interest include the South Asian diaspora, cultural diplomacy, Australia-India relations, and Bollywood. His research papers on these topics have appeared in high-ranking journals such as *Asian Ethnicity, Dance Chronicle, Dance Research, Antipodes, South Asian Popular Culture, South Asian Diaspora, Journalism Studies, Politics & Policy* and *Culture, Society and Masculinities*. He has many books to his credit, prominent being *Wanderings in India* (2012), *Bollywood and Its Other(s)* (2014), *Labels and Locations* (2015), *Salaam Bollywood* (2016), *South Asian Diaspora Narratives* (2016/2017), *Louise Lightfoot in Search of India* (2017) and *Vyakul Rashtra* (2017).

# The Dancing God
Staging Hindu Dance in Australia

**Amit Sarwal**

LONDON AND NEW YORK

First published 2020
by Routledge
2 Park Square, Milton Park, Abingdon, Oxon OX14 4RN

and by Routledge
52 Vanderbilt Avenue, New York, NY 10017

*Routledge is an imprint of the Taylor & Francis Group, an informa business*

First issued in paperback 2021

© 2020 Amit Sarwal

The right of Amit Sarwal to be identified as author of this work has been asserted by him in accordance with sections 77 and 78 of the Copyright, Designs and Patents Act 1988.

All rights reserved. No part of this book may be reprinted or reproduced or utilised in any form or by any electronic, mechanical, or other means, now known or hereafter invented, including photocopying and recording, or in any information storage or retrieval system, without permission in writing from the publishers.

*Trademark notice*: Product or corporate names may be trademarks or registered trademarks, and are used only for identification and explanation without intent to infringe.

*British Library Cataloguing-in-Publication Data*
A catalogue record for this book is available from the British Library

*Library of Congress Cataloging-in-Publication Data*
A catalog record has been requested for this book

ISBN: 978-0-367-26600-4 (hbk)
ISBN: 978-1-03-208597-5 (pbk)
ISBN: 978-0-429-29411-2 (ebk)

Typeset in Times New Roman
by Apex CoVantage, LLC

For Reema, Mishank and Saavi

# Contents

*List of figures* viii
*Glossary* xi
*Acknowledgements* xv

Introduction: the beginnings 1

1  Hindu, Hinduism and Hindutva 13

2  The Hindu dance 28

3  The Australian mother of Kathakali 54

4  The dancing God 78

Conclusion: temple dreaming 117

*Bibliography* 129
*Index* 143

# Figures

| | | |
|---|---|---|
| I.1 | Uday Shankar photographed as a *nautch* girl in Paris, c. 1930 | 3 |
| I.2 | Maharana Jagat Singh II and his *sardars* watching a *nautch* (1748); medium: opaque watercolour and gold paint on paper. Size: 48.6 × 32.2 cm (image) 56.3 × 40.0 cm (sheet) | 5 |
| I.3 | Ruth St Denis in *Radha*, ca 1906 | 6 |
| 1.1 | Mahatma Gandhi with Kasturba on their return to India from South Africa, 1915 | 20 |
| 1.2 | Vinayak Damodar Savarkar | 22 |
| 2.1 | Depiction of Hindu God Lord Shiva as Nataraj (God of Dance) in *Tandava*; copper alloy statue from tenth-century Chola Dynasty, Tamil Nadu, India, at the Los Angeles County Museum of Art | 29 |
| 2.2 | Cover of *Life* magazine featuring the Baroda Nautch Girls, Bombay, India, 1936 | 33 |
| 2.3 | Uday Shankar performing Gandharva dance, Paris, January 17, 1934 | 37 |
| 2.4 | Rukmini Devi in her 40s | 38 |
| 2.5 | Mahatma Gandhi with Pandit Jawaharlal Nehru and Khan Abdul Ghaffar Khan at the Asian Relations Conference in New Delhi, April, 1948 | 48 |
| 3.1 | Walter Burley Griffin and Marion Griffin in their garden at Castlecrag with architect Louise Lightfoot and Walter's father, George Griffin, 1927 | 55 |
| 3.2 | Anna Pavlova in *Oriental Impressions* (1923) | 57 |
| 3.3 | Louise Lightfoot and Misha Burlakov in *Dance Brutale* | 59 |
| 3.4 | Uday Shankar and Anna Pavlova in *Krishna and Radha*, ca. 1922 | 60 |

| | | |
|---|---|---|
| 3.5 | Bishop (Dr) George Arundale with his wife, Rukmini Devi Arundale, New South Wales, February 24, 1926 | 61 |
| 3.6 | Poster of *Coppelia* featuring Louise Lightfoot and Misha Burlakov, 1931 | 62 |
| 3.7 | Poster of *Walpurgis Night* and *Les Sylphides* featuring Louise Lightfoot and Misha Burlakov, 1932 | 64 |
| 3.8 | Rukmini Devi in a pose from Bharatanatyam | 68 |
| 3.9 | Gordon Hamilton and Colin McIntyre in First Australian Ballet's production of *The Blue God*, May 1938 | 69 |
| 3.10 | Louise Lightfoot and Ian C. Robson dancing on Europe Day at YWCA, Madras, India, 1938 | 72 |
| 3.11 | Louise Lightfoot wearing a sari | 73 |
| 4.1 | Ananda Shivaram, 1947 | 79 |
| 4.2 | Ananda Shivaram with his father and first guru, Gopala Panikar | 80 |
| 4.3 | Poet Vallathol Narayana Menon | 81 |
| 4.4 | Portrait of Indian dancer Ram Gopal, April 21, 1938 | 85 |
| 4.5 | An advertisement for a dance recital by Ananda Shivaram and Louise Lightfoot at the All India Khadi and Swadeshi Exhibition, Trichinopoly, India, 1939 | 87 |
| 4.6 | Ananda Shivaram received by Louise Lightfoot at Port Melbourne on board *SS Marella*, 1947 | 96 |
| 4.7 | Poster for Ananda Shivaram's first dance recital at the National Theatre, Melbourne, Victoria, April 28 to May 3, 1947 | 98 |
| 4.8 | Ananda Shivaram posing and performing eye exercises for Australian journalists, May 31, 1947 | 99 |
| 4.9 | Poster for Ananda Shivaram's dance recitals, 1947 | 102 |
| 4.10 | Ananda Shivaram in his iconic *Peacock Dance*, 1947 | 104 |
| 4.11 | Ananda Shivaram in a Man-Lion pose from *Narasimha Avatar*, 1947 | 106 |
| 4.12 | Poster for Ananda Shivaram's dance recital at Repertory Theatre, Perth, Western Australia, 1948 | 108 |
| 4.13 | Ananda Shivaram in *Ras Leela*, ca. 1940–1947 | 110 |
| 4.14 | Ruth Bergner, Ananda Shivaram and Louise Lightfoot, Fiji, 1950 | 112 |
| 5.1 | Shivarim [i.e.] Shivaram fans out his peacock plumage in an impromptu demonstration of Kathakali to Australian schoolchildren, 1974 | 118 |
| 5.2 | Louise Lightfoot and Yamini Krishnamurti at Swami Vishnudevananda's ashram near Montreal | 120 |

| | | |
|---|---|---|
| 5.3 | Louise Lightfoot with a Kathakali troupe from Kerala at Swami Vishnudevananda's ashram near Montreal | 121 |
| 5.4 | Louise Lightfoot, 1978 | 122 |
| 5.5 | Mary Louise Lightfoot; Dr Sunil Kothari; Tara Rajkumar, OAM; and Chandralekha at the performance of *Temple Dreaming* in Chennai, India, 1997 | 123 |
| 5.6 | A scene from *Temple Dreaming* choreographed by Tara Rajkumar, OAM, India, 1997 | 125 |

# Glossary

**abhinayas**   gesture language conveyed via hand-gestures and facial expressions to convey emotions and stories
**Adbhuta**   marvellous
**Advaita Vedanta**   a school in Hinduism
**Aharya**   dress
**Angika**   body gestures
**Anugraha**   salvation
**Aranyakas**   the philosophy behind ritual sacrifice in the Vedas
**asamyukta hastas**   single hand gestures
**Avirbhava**   creation
**bazaars**   markets
**bhagtans**   female dancers from the *bhagtan* community in Rajasthan
**Bhakti**   devotion
**Bhartiya shastriya nritya**   Indian classical dance
**Bhartiya shastriya sangeet**   Indian Classical Music
**bhava**   mood or feeling (accompanying *rasa*)
**Bhayanaka**   terrible
**bhramaris**   kinds of pirouettes
**Brahmanas**   commentaries on the Veda
**caris**   gaits
**chautal *(or* chartal*)***   four claps that are strongly linked to the *pakhawaj* (barrel-shaped drums) tradition
**chenda**   drum
**Dalits**   Untouchables or members of the lower castes
**Dasiattam**   a Dravidian dance
**devadasi**   a female servant of God who is dedicated to the temple deity
**Dvapara**   after two
**Guru**   teacher
**gurukulam**   literally, guru's house; also indicates a form of teaching where the student stays with the guru, learns the arts, and shares daily life

**Hasya**  comic
**Hindutva**  Hinduness
**idakka**  an hour-glass drum
**Isthiti**  preservation
**jatka**  a two-wheeled horse carriage
**jhaptal**  a ten beat or clap pattern used in raga exposition
**kalari**  gymnasium
**Kalaripayattu**  martial arts of Kerala
**kalavangtis**  women temple dancers
**Kali**  the age of darkness
**Kaliyogam**  Kathakali troupes
**kari**  black
**Karuna**  pathos
**Kathakali**  classical dance style from Kerala
**katti**  knife
**Krishnanattam**  Sanskrit plays in praise of Lord Krishna
**kriyas**  work of God
**Mahabharata**  one of the major Sanskrit epic narratives of India
**manasika**  the action of the mind
**mandalas**  universe or modes of standing
**manjira**  small cymbals
**matthas**  a Hindu monastery
**minukku**  radiant
**Mohiniattam**  a female classical Indian dance style from Kerala
**mridangam**  a drum played on the sides, used in South Indian Carnatic classical music
**mudras**  hand-gestures used both in abstract movement without any literal meaning and for symbolic meaning in telling stories and conveying emotions
**nagar badhus** (*or* **nagar vadhu**)  a courtesan
**Nair** (*or* **Nayar**)  an Indian caste in Kerala with matrilineal practices
**Nataraj**  the lord of dance with the iconic one leg raised up and pointing diagonally
**nattuvanar**  one who keeps the rhythmic beat (*talam*) in an Indian dance musical ensemble
**nautch**  a dance performed by professional dancing girls
**navarasas**  nine primary emotions (love, fear, laughter, valour, disgust, sorrow, anger, wonder, peace)
**Nayaka**  lord or hero
**nijbhasa**  a language of the individual and community
**nritta hastas**  ornate gestures
**nritta**  rhythmic footwork in traditional Indian dance

**Odissi** classical Indian dance style from the state of Orissa (Eastern India)
**pacca** green
**Pancakrtya** the five activities (production, maintenance, destruction, embodiment and release)
**Pandal** a temporary structure erected during Hindu religious festivals for worship and performance
**payuppu** ripe
**Prakriti** nature
**Puranas** Hindu religious texts that contain narratives about the history of the Universe from creation to destruction
**Purusha** omnipresent spirit
**Ramanattam** (*or* **Attakatha**) Malayalam plays in praise of Lord Rama
**rasa** emotion or taste
**Raudra** furious
**sabha** auditorium
**sahibs** elite Western visitors
**samhara** destruction
**samyukta hastas** combined hand gestures
**Santa** tranquil
**Saririka** bodily action
**Sattvika** physical
**Satya** the golden age
**Shaiva** followers of Shiva
**Shakta** followers of Devi
**shakti** female strength
**shuddha madalam** drum
**slokas** Sanskrit verse stanzas
**Smarta** followers of Brahman and all major deities
**Sringara** love expressed in various manifestations – romantic, erotic, motherly, divine
**sthankas** modes of resting
**Sutras** a rule or grammar of Hindu law and philosophy
**tāṇḍava** a divine dance performed by Lord Shiva
**tati** beard
**teppu** special
**Tirobhava** illusion
**Treta** the third age
**Upanishads** a collection of texts of religious, philosophical and historical nature
**utplavanas** kinds of leaps
**Vacka** vocal
**Vaishnava** followers of Vishnu

**Varanshrama Dharma** duties performed according to the Hindu system of social division and stages in life

**Vedas** texts of knowledge (the four *Vedas* are: *Rg Veda*, the *Samaveda*, *Yajurveda* and the *Atharvaveda*)

**Vibhatsa** disgust

**Vira** heroic

# Acknowledgements

Over the years, many people have made an impact on my life and work. Some of them I was able to meet, while others I was fortunate enough to work with in India, Australia and Fiji. The list far exceeds those whom I can name here. I wish to express my sincere thanks to everyone who has, directly or indirectly, made possible the writing of this book.

I would like to acknowledge the support of the Music Archives of Monash University. A very special thanks to Prof. Margaret Kartomi, Prof. Cat Hope, Dr Anthea Skinner, Bronia Kornhauser and Anubha Sarkar for providing me their valuable time, support and help in acquiring the material and permission to reprint a large number of images from the Louise Lightfoot Collection.

The copyright to Louise Lightfoot's writings and images is held by Mary Louise Lightfoot. Heartfelt thanks to Mary for granting her kind permission to reprint images in this book. I am also very grateful for her valuable suggestions and feedback during the writing process.

My gratitude to Tara Rajkumar, OAM, for her support of my work and for sharing the story behind her dance performance *Temple Dreaming*.

Thanks to the teams at the Library of Congress Prints and Photographs Division Washington, DC; the Kalashetra Foundation; the Indira Gandhi National Centre for the Arts; the Vallathol Museum; Swatantryaveer Savarkar Rashtriya Smarak; the National Library of Australia; the National Archives of Australia; and the National Gallery of Victoria for granting their kind permission to reprint some of the images from their archives. All reasonable efforts have been made to find the copyright owners of the works reproduced in this book. If you have any information about copyright, please contact Dr Amit Sarwal (sarwal.amit@gmail.com) or the Music Archives of Monash University.

I would also like to thank the people associated with the "Encounters: India" symposium (Brisbane, 2013) – Prof. Huib Schippers, Dr Helen Lancaster, Vincent Plush, and Rhiannon Phillips; the ADSA conference

(Adelaide, 2013) – Dr Maryrose Casey, Dr Sally Gardner, Michael Smalley and Nithya Nagarajan; and the ASAA conference (Perth, 2014) – Dr Kama Maclean. Many thanks to the editors and reviewers of the journal *Dance Chronicle* for their kind feedback on my article and permission to reprint it as a chapter here.

I am grateful to Prof. Dhananjay Singh and Dr Sakshi Chanana Thapa for their insightful comments and feedback on the first draft of my manuscript.

Sincerest thanks are also due to Prof. Pal Ahluwalia, Prof. Emerita Margaret Allen, Prof. Emeritus David Walker, Prof. David Lowe, Prof. Fethi Mansouri, Prof. Sudesh Mishra, Dr Sunil Kothari, Dr Mala Pandurang, Prof. Ashish Mohan Khokar and my colleagues at the University of Delhi, Deakin University, RMIT University and the University of the South Pacific for their support.

A special thanks to my friends Jitarth Jai Bharadwaj, Dr Mohit R. Pandit, Anjali Maindiratta, Harsha Sree, Vibhor Pandit, Shamsher Kainth, Ashrut Khatter, Hemesh Kumar, Karthik Arasu, Delys Paul, Prakash Elamakkara, Salvi Manish, Marshie Perera Rajkumar, Vijay Shinde, Parul Wadhwa and Gangotri Roy for helping me at various stages of the exhibition of my work.

Many thanks to Australian and Indian community media persons for covering and disseminating research related to the Louise Lightfoot project. Thanks also to the members of the Australia-India Interdisciplinary Research Network for their continuous support of my various endeavours in bringing India and Australia closer.

To the publishing team, especially Laura Hussey, for showing a keen interest in my book and commissioning this volume, and Laura Soppelsa, for working on it with professional skill and finesse, a very big thank you!

Thanks to my extended family in India, USA, Canada, and Germany for believing in my work and for their unconditional love. Last but certainly not least, I would like to express my most profound love, appreciation and thanks to my wife – Reema Sarwal; our children – Mishank Kansal Sarwal and Saavi Kansal Sarwal; my parents and parents-in-law – Virender Kumar Sarwal, Ranjana Sarwal, Devinder Kumar Kansal and Vandana Kansal; my brothers, brother-in-law and sisters-in-law – Anurag Sarwal, Mansi Nanda Sarwal, Rahul Sarwal, Veronica Sarwal, Aman Kansal and Vasudha Kansal.

I dedicate this book to my family, Louise Lightfoot, Mary Louise Lightfoot and all the artists of India and Australia.

**Dr. Amit Sarwal**
Suva, Fiji, 2019

# Introduction
## The beginnings

For many Australians, India has always been a land of mysticism, magic and moksha (spiritual emancipation); a land of "sahibs, sadhus and spinners"; or a land of "Jadoowallahs, Jugglers and Jinns," as the titles of 2009 and 2018 Australian books on India suggest.[1] Indian spirituality and philosophy, reflected through books such as *Bhagavad Gita*, has also captured the imagination of Australian intellectuals and writers alike. Further, there are many shared commonalities between the two countries – like the history of British imperialism, English language, trade and love of cricket. What is not popular knowledge is the fact that India was actually a lifeline for colonial Australia.[2] As a part of the British colonists' world, Australia made the first trade links with India. Recent sociological, anthropological and genetic studies have thrown light on linguistic similarities between Aborigines and Andamanese tribes. They also point to earlier links between pre-colonial Australia and the Indian subcontinent, such as the trade between Aborigines and Makassar seamen. Later, with the beginning of British colonialism in Australia, the Ghans and hawkers, who connected the outback with towns and cities, were brought from Northern India.[3] Eminent lawyer John Lang, who represented the Indian queen of Jhansi, Rani Lakshmibai, in court against the British, was the first Australian-born novelist.[4] The rum of the Rum Rebellion or Great Rebellion of 1808 came from India.[5] The popular and common habit of drinking tea, closely associated with British life in the tropics, came from India – an Australian named James "Rajah" Inglis made a fortune through his "Billy Tea" brand.[6] Similarly, in India, walers – the great horses of the British Raj used in Polo – were imported from New South Wales, and the Mahalaxmi Racecourse in Mumbai was designed after Caulfield and Randwick Racecourses. The last Nizam of Hyderabad made Western Australia his home for some time.[7] Owing to such connections, even today, some Australian towns and pastoral properties carry Indian names, reflecting a deep but sometimes fractured connection between colonial India and white Australia.[8]

## Introduction

A significant body of academic research on the *Immigration Restriction Act of 1901* or the White Australia Policy (henceforth WAP), unofficially in practice since the 1850s, has spanned the history of Asian migration and policy-making initiatives in Australia.[9] Prominent Australian scholars, such as Marie De Lepervanche,[10] David Walker,[11] Stuart Ward,[12] David Goldsworthy,[13] Margaret Allen[14] and Kama Maclean,[15] have also focused on the impact of the British Empire and WAP on early Australia-India relations in their research. According to Lyndon Megarrity, this was the most influential factor that dominated government policy formation and creation of perception in and about Australia.[16] This act prohibited anyone under a contract or agreement to perform manual labour from entering Australia and included a dictation test to assess skill in English (and a second language) of non-white persons.[17] The research on early Indians in the Australian colonies, especially Hindu and Punjabi settlements in New South Wales and Victoria, focused on male labourers, cameleers and plantation workers.[18] Because of the strict immigration policy and a dictation test, Indian women were excluded from entering Australia.[19] Post-1901, Indian and Australian intellectuals, policy-makers, journalists and diplomats made compelling arguments for productive collaborations between the two countries, especially in the fields of education, training and information exchange.[20] In the wake of prevailing ethos of equal rights among citizens of the British Empire, rising nationalism and the subsequent decline of the British Raj, Indian elites wanted to engage with Australia at the same level.[21] However, because of the existence of WAP, this engagement from the Australian side barely met the expectations of the Indian. This was, as pointed out earlier, substantiated by the strict immigration restrictions that furthered feelings of anti-colonialism amongst Indians.[22]

The Australian settler colonies – the white man's club – and India had a very different relationship to the British Empire.[23] This was often reflected in press stories and columns related to the inter-relations between the two colonies, as well as the treatment of Indians in Australia. Despite this fractured relationship, given the maritime and trade links between Australia and India, both nations attracted many curious and enthusiastic travellers.[24] In the mid-nineteenth century, at the great Intercolonial Exhibition of Australasia held in Melbourne (1866–1867), Australians had seen Indian curios, art products, colourful clothing, and paintings representing scenes of grand Indian palaces and *bazaars* (markets), along with travelling gipsy dancers from India.[25] During these early years of connection, Australians saw only visiting foreign dance and circus companies that performed full-length ballets and a vulgarised form of Hindu temple dance. These companies featured Asian and Indian people as exotic Oriental fantasies or freaks. These were shaped heavily by both colonial and anti-colonial discourses and dances made to represent the erotic sensuality and enlightened spirituality of India.[26]

Early Australian representations of Indian culture on stage and in radio productions, as well as in film and music, suffered from the influence of European imperial-colonial representations and the popular religio-culturalist constructs of India that resulted from the varied colonial encounters.[27] Sitara Thobani observes that one of the most recognisable images of a Hindu dancer was of the Hindu dancing girl – *devadasi* and *nautch* girls (Figure I.1).[28] Such *nautch* (dance) included aphrodisiac performances and erotic fantasy to satisfy the needs of spectators.[29] So, Australians who travelled to colonial India as *sahibs* (elite Western visitors) were primarily shown performances by such *nautch* girls – women "performing a shadow of degenerated forms of Kathak" in North Indian towns.[30] In Europe and the United States of America, the Hindu dance was reborn with white dancers.[31] The oriental dance and arts were mainly composed of exotic figures,

*Figure I.1* Uday Shankar photographed as a *nautch* girl in Paris, c. 1930

Photographer: P. Apors

Source: *A Century of Indian Dance, 1901–2000: The Mohan Khokar Dance Collection* (ICCR, 2011)

Photograph Courtesy: With one-time use permission of donor Ashish Khokar, Curator, Mohan Khokar Dance Collection, Indira Gandhi National Centre for the Arts

mysterious women, vibrant colours and elaborate temple or court designs (Figure I.2).[32]

Joan Erdman argues that the opportunity to promote oriental dance occurred in an environment of curiosity and unfamiliarity.[33] In the 1920s, many influential performers from the West – namely, Anna Pavlova,[34] Ruth St. Denis,[35] Ted Shawn,[36] Sol Hurok,[37] Esther Luella Sherman (a.k.a. Ragini Devi),[38] Martha Graham,[39] Jean Erdman[40] and La Meri[41] – turned to India and Hinduism for inspiration and experimentation (Figure I.3). Fernau Hall, a well-known dance critic for the *Daily Telegraph*, notes that the Indian (Hindu) temple dance made a strong impression on the Western world as early as AD 700 in Spain and then on nineteenth-century European ballet choreographers, who, unprepared to incorporate elements of Indian dance into ballet, restricted themselves to suggestive movements – unlike American choreographers of the twentieth century.[42] Erdman writes that once oriental dance became a popular genre, "created by western devotees with eastern ideas and values," the style influenced dancers in both Europe and the Orient.[43] Furthering this view, Prof. Ralph Yarrow observes that many of these practitioners felt something was "missing" or "lacking" from Western art and theatre – something "psychospiritual, technical, aesthetic or a combination of them all."[44] Here, Mary Louise Pratt's notion of the contact zone – "social spaces where cultures meet, clash, and grapple with each other, often in contexts of highly asymmetrical relations of power" becomes pertinent.[45] Like many of her European and American counterparts mentioned earlier, Louise Lightfoot decided to recreate Hindu dance pieces with her dance partner, Mischa Burlakov, for an Australian audience.

Prior to Louise Lightfoot's intervention, most theatrical novelties or ballet works performed in Sydney or Melbourne alluding to Indian settings, stories or characters were replete with exoticism and stereotypes aimed at Western audiences. Such works included ballets like *The Indian Maid* (1835) and *The Sultan's Choice* (1858) and the musical operas *A Moorish Maid* (1905), *The Golden Threshold* (1907), *Cora, the Temptress* (1915) and *The Rajah of Shivapore* (1917) – all "orientalist [spectacles] ready for consumption."[46] It is only much later in Australian music, particularly the jazz works of Bruce Clarke (1963) and Charlie Munro (1967) and the rock counterculture music of the group The Twilights (1968) and Terry Britten (1968), that there were some Indian influences and rhythms, a result of the universal popularity of Beatles.[47] Hence, Hindu or Indian classical dance in its vital form was virtually unseen and unknown in Australia, and Louise Lightfoot would play a major role in transforming this landscape.

This book has acquired shape through presentations of Louise Lightfoot's cross-cultural dance collaboration with Ananda Shivaram. It portrays the story of Hindu dance, often referred to as the Indian classical dance, in the

*Figure I.2* Maharana Jagat Singh II and his *sardars* watching a *nautch* (1748); medium: opaque watercolour and gold paint on paper; size: 48.6 × 32.2 cm (image) 56.3 × 40.0 cm (sheet)

Source: Photograph from the Felton Bequest, 1980 (AS142–1980)

Photograph Courtesy: National Gallery of Victoria, Melbourne

*Figure I.3* Ruth St Denis in *Radha*, ca 1906

Photographer: Aura Hartwig

Source: Mohan Khokar Dance Collection

Photograph Courtesy: With one-time use permission of donor Ashish Khokar, Curator, Mohan Khokar Dance Collection, Indira Gandhi National Centre for the Arts

context of Australia. Many books and research papers have been written and published on the history of Indian classical dance, reception of Indian classical dance outside India and dance personalities on the global stage. These have contributed immensely to the discipline of dance history. However, they have focused mostly on one dance form – that is, Bharatanatyam – and therefore could be supplemented by more research on other dance forms, like in this book. The story of the coming to prominence of Kathakali, a dance form deeply rooted in the sacred texts of Hinduism and temple dancing traditions, on the global stage has not been yet told in its entirety as well. It is my keen interest in Australia-India cross-cultural connections, rather than an attachment to the dance practice or form, that inspired me to begin a two-year postdoctoral research project in January 2013, titled "Cross-Cultural Diplomacy: Indian Visitors to Australia, 1947 to 1980," at Deakin University, Australia. While writing about the role of public diplomacy and cross-cultural perceptions in Australia-India relations, scholars have highlighted a shared history that underpins this relationship in all spheres.[48] Australian scholars have mostly focused on Australians gazing upon India.[49] But the other side of the coin, the building of early Indian perceptions of Australia, has largely been neglected in this discourse.[50] Margaret Allen has highlighted what educated and colonised Indian men, such as Otim Singh, Nunda Lall Doss and Sher Mahomed, visiting Australia in the late nineteenth and early twentieth century, felt about a colony of the same imperial power and the contemporary social, economic and imperial policies.[51]

My project was aimed at systematically examining how Australia and India viewed each other in the aftermath of decolonisation. It was particularly contextualised to key Indian visitors like noted dancers, journalists, writers and researchers from 1947 to 1980. During the research, I came to know about an Australian architect turned ballet teacher and impresario, Louise Lightfoot. In Australia, Louise was known for her Indian-Australian dance and cultural collaborations. In the late 1970s, before her death, Louise donated her life's work – handwritten notes, photographs, negatives, scrapbooks, sketches, press cuttings, programs, posters, brochures, letters, invoices, books, musical notes, maps, costumes, props and audio/video reels – in boxes and trunks, to the Music Archives of Monash University. These trunks are evidence of Louise's dedication and passion towards making the best dances and artists of the world accessible to the Australian audience. In connection with this project, I also accessed the music archives. At that time, my whole focus was on Indian dancers whose tours to Australia were organised by Louise Lightfoot, from 1947 to 1976. By the end of 2013, as I delved deeper into this archival collection, I realised that despite decades of hard work and dedication to Hindu dance and creating awareness about India in Australia, Louise's collaboration with these Indian artists was relatively unknown in both countries. With an aim to highlight Louise's work, in 2017, I compiled and edited her writing in a book entitled *In Search of India: An Australian Dancer's Experience.*[52]

Much of the work that I have carried out in my postdoctoral research at Deakin University (and after that as well) focused on two critical issues, which as a South Asian diaspora expert specialising in literature and cross-cultural relations, I am particularly interested in. The first is the de-provincialising of Hindu or Indian classical dance and second is the focus on Hindu or Indian classical dancers who saw themselves as cultural diplomats representing India on the global stage.

In this book, *The Dancing God: Staging Hindu Dance in Australia*, I have attempted to chart the sensational and fascinating journey of Indian classical dance in Australia. Using newspaper reports, advertisements, program brochures and Louise's journal entries related to the historic Australian tour of the first Indian dancer, Ananda Shivaram, I have analysed how this Hindu dance, a domain of the gods, transformed from the temples to the stage, giving rise to the figure of a global cultural ambassador.[53]

This book has been divided into four chapters. As this journey of dance from India to Australia is focused on Kathakali, the first chapter, "Hindu, Hinduism and Hindutva," provides a brief history of world's oldest religion and acquaints the readers with the key ideas governing the use of these three terms. As Hindu religion and its history is difficult to date and therefore a subject of much scholarly and public debate, I focus on the rise and revival of Hinduism and Hindutva, both in India and abroad. Chapter 2, "The Hindu Dance," introduces Kathakali, an integral part of the eleven reorganised dance forms often put in a composite category called *Bhartiya Shastriya Nritya* (Indian classical dance) by the government of India. This chapter presents how the traditional Hindu dance developed over the centuries with the help of both religious and local culture practices. It updates the readers on the many institutions revolving around the figure of women dancers, which have been common in India, especially the *devadasis*. It connects to the idea of *devadasis* and *nautch* girls who reached Australia from Europe and the United States of America. It also depicts how the abolishment of the *devadasi* system in 1947 was also the time when South Indian classical dances and institutions promoting them established their foothold in India and abroad.

Chapter 3, titled "The Australian Mother of Kathakali," traces Louise Lightfoot's journey from being a trained architect to a successful ballet teacher and later impresario for Indian dancers presenting varied classical dance forms around the world. It also showcases the brief history and performances of the Lightfoot-Burlakov school from 1929 to 1937. The highlight of this chapter is Louise's first impression of Uday Shankar's dance in

London, which made her move to Bombay and learn Indian classical dance so that she could bring more authenticity to her own ballet. The chapter then moves on to the next half-decade, when Louise lived in Kerala and Tamil Nadu to learn the different techniques of the sacred dance styles Kathakali and Bharatanatyam. It concludes with Louise's realisation and resolve to present this difficult and intricate dance subject to Australians in her unique way.

Chapter 4, titled "The Dancing God," recounts the performance of the first Hindu artist to tour Australia in 1947. Ananda Shivaram, the renowned Kathakali dancer and teacher, with his unique and expressive style, was celebrated as a star and visiting cultural ambassador to Australia. The chapter begins in 1938, when Lightfoot first met Shivaram at the Kerala Kalamandalam. The chapter throws some light on his early life, family and dance training. It also shows how, until the arrival of Louise, it had been difficult for him to arrange for a solo tour of Western countries. Louise's guidance and experience in running a tour company enabled Shivaram to form his own dance company and stage Hindu dance abroad. It goes on to delineate how Louise persuaded Shivaram to experiment, create shorter versions of dance-dramas and adapt ancient Kathakali works to modern tastes with her Hindu Dance Group in Australia. It was with Louise's support and guidance that Shivaram was able to redefine a previously unseen dance form – Kathakali – and help the foreign audience to grasp the secrets of the gestural language and the intricacies of body movement. Although well-liked within the dance world of Australia, Shivaram's tryst with racial prejudice was obvious and hence forms a part of the chapter. The chapter concludes with Shivaram's other tours to Australia and his impressions of Australia and its people.

In the concluding chapter, "Temple Dreaming," I argue that it must have been a great challenge for a Kathakali dancer to tamper with the age-old tradition. However, Louise, along with Shivaram, was successful in experimenting with and promoting a range of Hindu dance forms. Here, I briefly also trace the final journey of Louise through a dance project entitled *Temple Dreaming* created by Tara Rajkumar, OAM. This was a much celebrated tribute to Louise's and other multicultural dance performances that became possible because of her experiments and initiatives.

This book, as pointed out earlier, is the story of the making of a renowned Indian exponent and cultural ambassador of the Kathakali dance form on the world stage. The eminent critics of Indian dance have argued that such international exposure provided dignity to both the Indian classical dance and dancers, emerging from a long period of European domination and humiliation. I hope that the story in this book will prompt further publications on traditional Hindu dance and Australia-India contemporary dance connections.

## Notes

1. Bennett et al., *Of Sadhus and Spinners*, 2009; Zubrzycki, *Jadoowallahs, Jugglers and Jinns*, 2018 (this book was first published as *Empire of Enchantment: The Story of Indian Magic* by Scribe).
2. Sarwal, *South Asian Diaspora Narratives*, 2016.
3. The Afghans or Ghans were cameleers who worked in the Australian outback prominently from the 1860s to the 1930s. See "Afghan Cameleers in Australia," 2009. For a detailed discussion on Ghans and camelmen, see Rajkowski, *In the Tracks of the Camelmen*, 1987; Khatun, *Australianama*, 2018.
4. Refer to Earnshaw, "Lang, John (1816–1864)," 1974; Medcalf, "John Lang, Our Forgotten Indian Envoy," 2010.
5. Darwin, *Unfinished Empire*, 2012.
6. On James Inglis, see Rutledge, "Inglis, James (1845–1908)," 1972; Walker, *Anxious Nation*, 1999.
7. Zubrzycki, *The Last Nizam*, 2006.
8. For a discussion on colonial connections between Australia and India, see Walker, *Anxious Nation*, 1999; Westrip and Holroyde, *Colonial Cousins*, 2010; Bayly, "India and Australia," 2012.
9. For a detailed discussion on the White Australia Policy, see Willard, *History of the White Australia Policy to 1920*, 1923; Walker, *Anxious Nation*, 1999; Tavan, *The Long, Slow Death of White Australia*, 2005.
10. De Lepervanche, *Indians in a White Australia*, 1984.
11. See Walker, *Anxious Nation*, 1999; Walker, "National Narratives," 2002.
12. Ward, *Australia and the British Embrace*, 2001.
13. Goldsworthy, *Losing the Blanket*, 2002.
14. See Allen, "'Innocents Abroad' and 'Prohibited Immigrants'," 2005; Allen, "'A Fine Type of Hindoo' Meets 'the Australian Type'," 2008; Allen, "Shadow Letters and the Karnana Letter," 2011; Allen, "I Am a British Subject," 2018.
15. Maclean, "Examinations, Access, and Inequity Within the Empire," 2015.
16. Megarrity, "Regional Goodwill, Sensibly Priced," 105.
17. For a discussion on immigration restrictions and its impact, see Allen, "'Innocents Abroad' and 'Prohibited Immigrants'," 2005; Maclean, "Examinations, Access, and Inequity Within the Empire," 2015.
18. On Hindu and Punjabi settlement in Australia, see Bilimoria, "Speaking of the Hindu Diaspora in Australia," 1998; Bilimoria et al., *The Indian Diaspora*, 2015.
19. For a discussion on South Asian migration, see Allen, "Shadow Letters and the Karnana Letter," 2011; De Lepervanche, "The (Silent) Voices of Indian Colies," 2013; Sarwal, *South Asian Diaspora Narratives*, 2016; Sarwal, *Labels and Locations*, 2015.
20. Sarwal, "A Kangaroo and Bradman," 2018.
21. Allen, "I Am a British Subject," 2018.
22. On the impact of strict immigration restrictions on British subjects, see Maclean, "Examinations, Access, and Inequity Within the Empire," 2015; Frost, "Imperial Citizenship or Else," 2018.
23. Refer to Ahmed, "India's Membership of the Commonwealth: Nehru's Role," 1991; Walker, *Anxious Nation*, 1999; Broinowski, *About Face*, 2003; Bayly, "India and Australia," 2012.
24. For a discussion on various travellers, see Bilimoria, "Speaking of the Hindu Diaspora in Australia," 1998; Allen, "'Innocents Abroad' and 'Prohibited

Immigrants'," 2005; Allen, "'A Fine Type of Hindoo' Meets 'the Australian Type'," 2008.
25 Through the Intercolonial Exhibition, which opened on 24 October 1866 and closed on 23 February 1867, for the first time, the Australian colonies came together. See "Melbourne: Intercolonial Exhibition of Australasia 1866–67," 2017.
26 Thobani, *Indian Classical Dance and the Making of Postcolonial National Identities*, 147.
27 For a discussion on varied colonial encounters and the influence of European imperial-colonial representations, see Scott-Maxwell, "Asia and Pacific Links," 54; Broinowski, *The Yellow Lady*, 1996; Walker, *Anxious Nation*, 1999; Bilimoria, "Indian Dance," 2003; Bilimoria, "The Spiritual Transformation of Indian Dance in Australia," 2008; Thobani, *Indian Classical Dance and the Making of Postcolonial National Identities*, 147.
28 Thobani, *Indian Classical Dance and the Making of Postcolonial National Identities*, 2017.
29 Hanna, *Dance, Sex, and Gender*, 1988.
30 Coorlawala, "Ruth St. Denis and India's Dance Renaissance," 130.
31 Srinivasan, *Sweating Saris*, 63–64.
32 Erdman, "Dance Discourses," 1996.
33 Ibid.
34 Anna Pavlova was a well-known Russian prima ballerina of the late nineteenth and the early twentieth centuries. Pavlova was a principal artist of the Imperial Russian Ballet and the Ballets Russes. She is the most recognised for the creation of the role *The Dying Swan*. See Dandré, *Anna Pavlova*, 1932/1979; Sorell, *Dance in Its Time*, 1986.
35 Ruth St. Denis was an American contemporary dance innovator. In 1906, after studying Hindu dance, art and philosophy, Ruth offered a public performance in New York City of her first dance work – *Radha*. In her later tours, she also added *The Nautch* and *The Yogi* to her dance program. See Desmond, "Dancing out the Difference," 256–70.
36 Ted Shawn (born Edwin Myers Shawn) was one of the pioneers of American modern dance. He created Denishawn with his former wife, Ruth St. Denis. In 1926, Shawn created "The Cosmic Dance of Shiva." See Terry, *Ted Shawn*, 1976.
37 Sol Hurok was a twentieth-century American dance impresario who managed well-known performing artists. See Robinson, *The Last Impresario*, 1994.
38 Ragini Devi made her impact on Indian classical dance and stage even before Rukmini Devi and Sri Vallathol. See Devi, *Dance Dialects of India*, 1990; Rahman, *Dancing in the Family*, 2002; Sen, "Return of the Prodigy," 1976.
39 Martha Graham was an American modern dancer and choreographer. Her style is known as the "Graham technique," which reshaped American dance. See Horosko, *Martha Graham*, 2002.
40 Jean Erdman is an American dancer, choreographer and theatre director.
41 La Meri was an American dancer, choreographer, teacher, poet, anthropologist and scholar. In the 1930s, La Meri invited Indian classical dance guru Ram Gopal to tour with her extensively in the West. See Au and Rutter, *Ballet and Modern Dance*, 2012.
42 For a discussion on incorporation of elements of Indian dance into ballet, see Hall, "The Contribution of Indian Dance to British Culture," 1982; Bilimoria, "Traditions and Transition in South Asian Performing Arts in Multicultural Australia," 115.

43 Erdman, "Dance Discourses," 1996.
44 Yarrow, *Indian Theatre*, 16.
45 Pratt, "Arts of the Contact Zone," 34.
46 Srinivasan, *Sweating Saris*, 142.
47 For a detailed discussion of exoticism and stereotypes, see Broinowski, *The Yellow Lady*, 1996; Walker, *Anxious Nation*, 1999; Scott-Maxwell, "Asia and Pacific Links," 2003; Bilimoria, "Indian Dance," 330–31.
48 Davis, "A Shared History?" 849–69.
49 For a discussion of Australian perceptions of India, see Hosking and Sarwal, *Wanderings in India*, 2012; Walker and Sobocinska, *Australia's Asia*, 2012; Walker, "National Narratives," 2002; Walker, *Experiencing Turbulence*, 2013.
50 For a discussion of Indian perceptions of Australia, see De Lepervanche, *Indians in a White Australia*, 1984; Maclean, "India in Australia," 2012.
51 For a detailed discussion of Otim Singh, Nunda Lall Doss and Sher Mahomed, see Allen, "Observing Australia as the 'Member of an Alien and Conquered Race'," 2009a; Allen, "Otim Singh in White Australia," 2009b; Allen, "Identifying Sher Mohamad," 2013.
52 Sarwal, *In Search of India*, 2017.
53 Louise Lightfoot's journal entries and notes on her visit to India were meant to be published as an adventure book. Louise's niece Mary Louise Lightfoot published this account with her own commentary and research in a beautiful book entitled *Lightfoot Dancing: An Australian-Indian Affair* (2015).

# 1 Hindu, Hinduism and Hindutva[1]

As mentioned in the introduction, in Europe and the United States of America, the "Hindu temple dance" was reborn with predominantly "white dancers."[2] Even in the case of Louise Lightfoot, she first introduced Kathakali dance to Australia with the Hindu tradition of temple dancing as the point of reference – famously called Hindu dance.[3] Her own dance group in Australia was named the Hindu Dance Group, and as an impresario, Louise's interest was in presenting authentic Hindu culture and art to an Australian audience.[4] So, my starting point as an interdisciplinary scholar specialising in literature and cross-cultural relations is comprehending the nuances of being Hindu, Hinduism in Kerala, Hindu dance, and the interrelationship between religion and art in India. The words *Hindu*, *Hinduism* and *Hindutva* have today come to possess a unique attraction and have become a recurrent topic in a variety of forum discussions in both India and abroad. Without getting caught up in the controversies surrounding the recent debates on Hindutva, a term that has been, since the 1990s, widely used for the resurgence of Hindu nationalism in India,[5] let us start with the idea of Hindu and Hinduism.[6]

The scholars specialising in the history of the Hindu religion and tradition claim it to be the world's oldest religion based on textual evidence from the *Rg Veda*.[7] The pertinent question here is – did the Hindu religious traditions arise in the Indus Valley civilisation? Or did they come with the Vedic Aryans?[8] With reference to the development of Hinduism, there have been two major theories, namely, the Aryan invasion theory and the cultural transformation theory. According to the first theory, Aryans invaded, and their religious texts – the *Vedas* – became dominant in the Indian sub-continent. The second theory interprets Aryan culture and sacred texts as part of a development narrative of the Indus Valley culture.[9] As the Hindus did not believe in the linearity of time, a notion colonialism brought to them, exact dates are unavailable. However, periods of their history have been logically inferred from textual references. This proves the fact that Hinduism has

14  *Hindu, Hinduism and Hindutva*

existed in India as a belief system and an unbroken intellectual tradition over the past three thousand years. Unlike the Abrahamic religions, Hinduism is not a single religion; rather, it embraces many ancient traditions and philosophies and therefore goes back several thousand years. In fact, it is no religion in the Abrahamic sense. There is no single reference book to practice the belief systems, which are diverse and often contradictory to one another. The word *dharma* that the Hindus use typically refers to their spiritual practice as well as daily ethical living and denotes righteousness of thought and action.

Scottish historian and philosopher James Mill, in his *The History of British India*, distinguished three phases in the history of India, namely Hindu, Muslim and British civilisations.[10] This is a very simple division of a problematic time line. The following time line presents a brief but elaborate chronology of the development of Hinduism in India:

- Up to 2000 BCE: The Indus Valley civilisation
- 1500 BCE to 500 BCE: The Vedic period
- 500 BCE to 500 CE: The Epics, Puranic and Classical Age
- 500 CE to 1500 CE: Medieval Period and Islamic invasion
- 1500 CE to 1757 CE: Pre-modern period and Bhakti Movement
- 1757 CE to 1947 CE: British period, Hindu renaissance and the emergence of the Hindutva ideology
- 1947 CE to the present: Independent India and Hindutva ideology in politics

Sharada Sugirtharajah, in her book *Imagining Hinduism*, has argued that Hinduism has been a central feature in "Western consciousness" and redefined mostly in "Western categories."[11] While Romila Thapar and Arvind Sharma have highlighted scholarly attempts that have been made to trace parallels of India's (Hindu) past with Biblical theories and the rise of these terms in a Hindu-Muslim polarity.[12] This is similar to the views of Welsh orientalist William Jones, who, in 1799, pointed to the close resemblance between the classical languages of Europe and Sanskrit and declared that the four Hindu *yugas* (ages) – *Satya* or *Krita*, *Treta*, *Dvapara*, and *Kali* – have affinity with Roman and Grecian ages. He placed the idea of Hindu *yugas* within a biblical framework based on common or similar theistic practices. Jones observed,

> We may here observe, that the true History of the World seems obviously divisible into four ages or periods; which may be called, the first, the *Diluvian*, or purest age; namely the times preceding the deluge . . . next, the *Patriarchal*, or pure age; in which, indeed, there were mighty

hunters of beasts and men, . . . – Thirdly, the *Mosaick*, or less pure age; from the legation of Moses, and during this time when his ordinances were comparatively well observed and uncorrupted – Lastly, the *Prophetical*, or impure age; beginning with the vehement warnings given by the Prophets to apostate Kings and degenerate nations, but still subsiding and to subsist, until all genuine prophecies shall be fully accomplished.[13]

For Jones, looking from a Biblical lens, Hinduism was an "erroneous religion" which had more to do with imagination than reason.[14]

So, are *Hindu* and *Hinduism* misleading terms? Hinduism, the religion, is a tradition that encompasses various ideas – from the Vedic to present-day thoughts and values. The Vedic period, which was from 1500 to 500 BCE, is now known for the composition of the ritual texts, the epics, the *Sutras*, the *Brahmanas*, the *Aranyakas*, the *Upanishads* and chiefly the four *Vedas* – the *Rg Veda*, the *Samaveda*, *Yajurveda* and the *Atharvaveda*. But the term *Hindu*, post-Vedic period, originally comes from the Sanskrit word *Sindhu* (Sindhu River or Indus River), the region of the cultures of the Indus Valley civilisation (2500–1500 BCE).[15] These people, in some ways, may have been related to the Dravidians in South India, but it is still debatable, as the script and writing have yet to be deciphered.[16] J. Brockington in *The Sacred Thread* comments, "it must not be forgotten that the religion of the Vedas was an alien culture brought into India by the Aryans."[17] The theory of an Aryan presence in India before the Indus Valley Civilisation has not been fully validated and has been debunked by some scholars and historians.[18] In fact, in 1914, Sri Aurobindo discredited this theory by pointing to the exaggerated, overstated and superficial claims made in the nineteenth century by comparative philologists in favour of the linguistic commonality between the Aryan tongue and the Sanskrit language.

> The first error committed by the philologists after their momentous discovery of the Sanskrit tongue, was to exaggerate the importance of their first superficial discoveries. The first glance is apt to be superficial; the perceptions drawn from an initial survey stand always in need of correction. If then we are so dazzled and led away by them as to make them the very key of our future knowledge, its central plank, its bacic platform we prepare ourselves grievous disappointments. Comparative Philology, guilty of this error, has seized on a minor clue and mistaken it for a major or chief clue.[19]

Debate continues on the myths of the origins of India and Hinduism, particularly about the extent of fusion of Aryan and Dravidian traditions.

Noted Indian historian Romila Thapar, in her article "The Theory of Aryan Race and India," has shown how Aryan theory started as an attempt to uncover the beginnings of Indian history and explain the society's mythical origins.[20] With it as a framework, the roots of an Indian identity were established and later used in Hindutva politics.[21] The upper-caste Hindus have used the Aryan theory to prove their superiority to indigenous populations of India and equality to Europeans. Scholars belonging to or sympathising with the lower-castes in India and abroad have used it to provide "the Dalit version of history."[22]

Scholars of Hinduism have also argued elsewhere that the term *Hindu* was mostly used by Persians or Muslim conquerors to refer to the inhabitants of the areas near the Indus River and not to any religious denomination. According to A. V. Williams Jackson, the earliest known use of the word *Hindu* appears in the sacred book of Zoroastrianism – *Zend Avesta*:

> The first chapter of the Avestan Vendidad (whatever may be the age of the chapter) contains an allusion to a portion of Northern India in a list which it gives of sixteen lands or regions, created by Ahur Mazda and apparently regarded as under Iranian sway. The fifteenth of these domains, according to Vd. 1, 18 was Hapta Hindu, "Seven Rivers", a region of "abnormal heat", probably identical with the territory of Sapta Sindhavas, "Seven Rivers", in the Veda (see especially Rv. VIII, 24, 27)[23]

With travellers coming from Greece, China and Arabia, Sindhu (or Sindh) became "India," "Indu" and "al-Hind," thus acquiring territorial and religious references respectively.[24] But this idea of India was still confined to Sindh (North), and under the prevalent definitions of Indian philosophy, being a Hindu was not a way of religious thinking but a way of life, say, as opposed to an Islamic one.[25] Aziz Ahmad has also pointed to the significance of the Arab conquest of Sind c.712 and its impact on creating this idea of Hindus as a category for both religious and administrative purposes:

> The conquest of Sind by Muhammad ibn Qasim, and the incorporation of that province into the Muslim universal caliphate, brought the Muslims there in a relationship of a very different nature, that of the ruled and the ruler. This form of political relationship, which some centuries later extended to the whole sub-continent, and survived until well into the eighteenth century inevitably led to the creation of tensions which determined very largely the psychological course of the history of medieval and modern India.[26]

The conquest brought about the acceptance and borrowing of the victor's language. This India, in the intriguing words of famous scholar and traveller Alberuni (Al-Biruni), was a religious antagonist of Islam.[27] Alberuni writes,

> Another circumstance which increased the already existing antagonism between Hindus and foreigners is that the so-called Shamaniyya (Buddhists), though they cordially hate Brahmans, still are nearer akin to them than to others. In former times, Khurdsdn, Persis, Irak, Mosul, the country up to the frontier of Syria, was Buddhistic, but then Zarathustra went forth from Adharbaijan and preached Magism in Balkh (Baktra). His doctrine came into favour with King Gushtasp, and his son Isfendiyad spread the new faith both in east and west, both by force and by treaties. He founded fire-temples through his whole empire, from the frontiers of China to those of the Greek empire. The succeeding kings made their religion (i.e. Zoroastrianism) the obligatory state-religion for Persis and Irak. In consequence, the Buddhists were banished from those countries and had to emigrate to the countries east of Balk.[28]

Richard H. Davis has described Alberuni's account of India and Hindus as moving between a centralist (based in the hegemony of Sanskrit texts and Vedic mythology) and pluralist (tolerance and incorporation of all ideas) views of approaching Hinduism.[29] Hindus through various sects – *Shaiva* (followers of Shiva), *Vaishnava* (followers of Vishnu), *Shakta* (followers of Devi) and *Smarta* (followers of Brahman and all major deities) – believe that all the deities are a manifestation of one. Eminent Sanskrit scholar J. A. B. van Buitenen, in the *Encyclopedia Britannica*, defined Hinduism in context of its pluralistic ideals:

> In principle, Hinduism incorporates all forms of belief and worship without necessitating the selection or elimination of any. The Hindu is inclined to revere the divinity in every manifestation, whatever it may be, and is doctrinally tolerant . . . Hinduism is, then, both a civilization and a conglomeration of religions, with neither a beginning, a founder, nor a central authority, hierarchy, or organization.[30]

By the thirteenth century, the word *Hindu* gave rise to another word – *Hindustan*. This literally meant "the land of the Hindus" and became synonymous with North India.[31] Here, amalgamation of all religions – Islam, Buddhism, Sikhism and Sufism – influenced North Indian culture. However, the original Vedic traditions remained well-preserved in South India, especially in Tamil Nadu and Kerala, where classical literature and epics were written in Dravidian languages (such as Tamil and Malayalam), and Sanskrit made continuous references to Vedic gods and culture.[32]

Over the centuries, Hinduism in South Indian states developed with its own distinctive socio-cultural mores and systems of philosophical inquiry.[33] Kerala's culture, where Kathakali dance-drama was born, is firmly rooted in the *Vedas*. Historical studies on Hinduism or Sanathana Dharma in Kerala include practices transmitted down from Vedic Brahmanism and ancient Dravidian beliefs, as well as devotional traditions of the medieval period, especially rituals and performances.[34] Adi Shankara, one of the most famous Hindu saints, scholars and philosophers, who consolidated the doctrine of *Advaita Vedanta*, was from Kerala. He established four *matthas* (Hindu monasteries) at Sringeri, Dwarka, Puri and Jyotirmath. Hindus in Kerala worshipped different cults of Lord Shiva and Lord Vishnu in addition to the goddess Bhagavathi (a form of Shakti). Robin Jeffrey writes,

> In the last half of the 19th century a society which had survived fundamentally unchanged for 700 years came unhinged. A movement from inherited to achieved status began, a movement from the interdependence of castes to the competition of individuals, from traditional authority to modern bureaucracy.[35]

According to this view, until the arrival of the British, Kerala was a static society in terms of preservation of its socio-cultural and religious traditions. But Susan Bayly does not agree with this view and points to the period in the eighteenth century, when the Kerala society underwent radical changes in the political system, especially Keralan rulers' religious policies, which became "fluid and syncretic."[36] They displayed none of the adherence to Malayali Hindu orthodoxy and often explored the strategies of state building by recruiting Hindu warriors from outside Kerala.[37] She further argues that many of the forms which are now considered to be traditional in Kerala Hindu society are "actually products of collapse and disintegration in the eighteenth-century."[38]

Thapar writes that it was only by the fifteenth and sixteenth centuries that the word *Hindu* was formally appropriated by Hindus themselves. This happened under the influence of the *Bhakti* movement (theistic devotional movement) to distinguish the Hindu community from Muslims.[39] Orientalist scholars such as H. H. Wilson, M. Monier-Williams and G. A. Grierson compared *Bhakti* to a monotheistic reform movement, almost at the level of Protestant Christianity, particularly with its focus on one god – Lord Vishnu – and its criticism of caste.[40] There are many images and interpretations of the *Bhakti* movement as it works on a complex structure of complex participation.[41] Hinduism, with the emergence of *Bhakti* tradition and its sub-religion Vaishnavism (devotion to Lord Vishnu and his incarnation Lord Krishna), in fact, had a far-reaching impact on Indian society, literature, art and dance.

With the coming of the British, the word *Hindu* began to be used as an umbrella term "to characterize all things in India."[42] Wilfred Cantwell Smith, in *Meaning and End of Religion*, has also observed that the use of the word *Hindu* in the meaning "Indian" survived in popular English into the twentieth century.[43] The term *Hindu* in the eighteenth and nineteenth century predominantly came to be associated with a religious identity of the people of India, just like *Christian* and *Muslim*, by the British administrators. In this context, Sugirtharajah observes that it was the Orientalists who categorised and compartmentalised India, Hinduism, the sacred texts and Sanskrit language. She writes,

> Orientalists saw themselves as "discovering" India's ancient past and as enlightening the Hindu elite with their newly discovered knowledge. Orientalists, in studying the ancient Sanskrit texts, came to textualize, restructure, and domesticate them.[44]

Among Hindus, the Young Bengal Group in the 1840s at Calcutta (now Kolkata) saw itself as a collection of reformers and talked of the Hindus and Hinduism critically. For these Hindu reformers, a purified Hinduism meant a socio-religious practice that can correspond to universal values.[45] By the end of the nineteenth century, Indian modernists, such as Raja Rammohan Roy, Sri Aurobindo and Swami Vivekananda,[46] had helped in purifying Hinduism by elevating the Vedic elements and creating the global appeal of its philosophies.[47]

Once this process of reform of Hinduism was over, it was only in the twentieth century that the term *Hindu* was reconstructed and associated with the emergence of Hindutva as a political force and a source of national identity in India. It can be argued that the neo-Vedanta indirectly contributed to the Hindutva ideology and politics. Even Mahatma Gandhi, leader of the Indian National Congress (INC), called himself a *Sanatani* Hindu, because of his strong belief in the *Vedas*, the *Upanishads*, the *Puranas*, the *Varanshrama Dharma* and the protection of the cow (Figure 1.1).[48] In the 1920s, Gandhi focussed on Hinduism, not as an exclusive or a missionary religion, but as one which was all-encompassing and peaceful. In an article published in *Young India*, he writes,

> Believing as I do in the influence of heredity, being born in a Hindu family, I have remained a Hindu. I should reject it, if I found it inconsistent with my moral sense or my spiritual growth. On examination,

*Figure 1.1* Mahatma Gandhi with Kasturba on their return to India from South Africa, 1915

Photograph: Press Information Bureau, Government of India
Collection: Gandhi Photos, 1886–1948
Source: https://digicoll.manoa.hawaii.edu
Photograph Courtesy: University of Hawaii

I have found it to be the most tolerant of all religions known to me. Its freedom from dogma makes a forcible appeal to me inasmuch as it gives the votary the largest scope for self-expression. Not being an exclusive religion, it enables the followers of that faith not merely to respect all the other religions, but it also enables them to admire and assimilate whatever may be good in the other faiths. Non-violence is common to all religions, but it has found the highest expression and application in Hinduism. (I do not regard Jainism or Buddhism as separate from Hinduism.) Hinduism believes in the oneness not of merely all human life but in the oneness of all that lives. Its worship of the cow is, in my opinion, its unique contribution to the evolution of humanitarianism. It is a practical application of the belief in the oneness and, therefore, sacredness, of all life. The great belief in transmigration is a direct consequence of that belief. Finally, the discovery of the law of *Varnashrama* is a magnificent result of the ceaseless search for truth.[49]

Some believed that there was an ambiguity in Gandhi's "soft Hinduism" that resulted in communal conflicts and dissatisfaction among Muslims and Dalits in the 1920s and onwards. David Page, discussing the communal conflict of the 1920s, observes how the political reforms of 1919 "gave way to communal antagonism."[50] Many Congress workers and leaders, in the 1930s and 1940s, often identified with the idea of a "Hindu nation" acknowledging the fluidity of the term then taken as a secular nation for all,[51] an idea that was promoted by Gandhi's contemporary, Vinayak Damodar Savarkar. This idea for a Hindu nation was based on a form of militant Hinduism (Figure 1.2).

Savarkar believed that the competition between Hindu and Muslim communities only served as the basis for hatred and that this divisiveness could only be cured if Indians were either able to identify themselves as "Hindu," or there was a provision for two-states – Hindu and Muslim.[52] Savarkar coined the term *Hindutva* (Hinduness) in his 1923 pamphlet entitled *Hindutva: Who Is a Hindu?*[53] His work was published at a time when Indian nationalism and the independence movement were on the rise and was marginally promoted as an idea of a nationalised Hinduism or a "Hindu Rashtra" (a Hindu nation) tied together by blood, consciousness and ancient land.[54] Savarkar writes,

> We Hindus are bound together not only by the tie of the love we bear to a common fatherland and by the common blood that courses through our veins and keeps our hearts throbbing and our affections warm, but also by the tie of the common homage we pay to our great civilization – our Hindu culture.[55]

*Figure 1.2* Vinayak Damodar Savarkar
Photographer: Unknown
Source: Public Domain
Photograph Courtesy: Swatantryaveer Savarkar Rashtriya Smarak

However, being a Hindu (the religion) and adhering to Hindutva ideals (the ideology) were two different things. For Savarkar, Hinduism was a religion with many sub-sects, belief systems and traditions, and his idea of Hindutva was based on a political and nationalistic ideology highlighting all Indians, regardless of their religious identities, as "Hindus" because of the geographical construct or a unifying geographical boundary.

In his pamphlet, Savarkar approached the question through both the religious and historical lens, focusing on people living in the nation of India as Hindu people with one ethnic, cultural and political identity. Janaki Bakhle places Savarkar among the four most important anticolonial nationalists along with Mahatma Gandhi, Pundit Jawaharlal Nehru and Netaji Subash Chandra Bose.[56] His political ideology of Hindutva, as has been noted by Sumanta Banerjee, was based on a combination of received tradition, history and mythology and an active refashioning of this tradition to exercise authority.[57] This model then, it can be argued, was based on absolute authoritarian inferences and didn't actually address India's social, cultural and economic conflicts.[58] Ashis Nandy has observed that Savarkar's ideology influenced sections of urban, middle-class, modernising Hindus of British India.[59] He, in turn, Nandy observes, was influenced by Brahmabandhav Upadhyay, a Catholic theologian, Vedantic scholar and pioneer in indigenous Christian theology.[60] Upadhyay was also a Hindu nationalist scholar-activist whose political Hinduism finally ended up as Savarkar's Hindutva.[61] In the 1940s, the Muslim League leader Mohammad Ali Jinnah proposed his two-nation theory based on the Hindu-Muslim divide. Savarkar declared on August 15, 1943, "I have no quarrel with Mr Jinnah's two-nation theory. We Hindus are a nation by ourselves and it is a historical fact that Hindus and Muslims are two nations."[62] But post-independence, Savarkar's life became controversial because of his role in Mahatma Gandhi's murder and his letters promising loyalty to the British authorities.[63] The glorification of Savarkar's ideology by the Rashtriya Swayamsevak Sangh (RSS; formed in the 1920s), the Vishwa Hindu Parishad (VHP; formed in the 1960s), the Shiv Sena (formed in the 1960s) and the Bharatiya Janata Party (BJP; formed in the 1970s) facilitate the internalisation of the political force of Indian nationalism.[64] For these religious-political groups, the philosophy of Hindutva is grounded in a supposedly common agreement established on the basis of a common Hindu identity, which therefore leaves out any other way of life or belief system, such as those of Muslims or Christians.[65]

Today, Savarkar's ideology of Hindutva has attained legitimacy in India, the world's largest secular democracy, and some critics label the rise of the BJP as "Hindu fundamentalism."[66] Given India's political landscape and ideological mimicking by both national- and regional-level parties, I do not adhere to the qualification "Hindu communalism" or "Hindu fundamentalism." It is apparent now that, with the changing political landscape, notions drawn from Congress's "soft Hindutva" of the 1930s and 1940s are being re-employed.[67] Two recent events – the visit of Congress President Rahul Gandhi to almost all popular Hindu temples to prove his identity as a "Hindu" and publication of *Why I Am a Hindu* by senior Congress leader and well-known author Shashi Tharoor – have demonstrated the ease with which Congress can appeal to and persuade voters based on its own brand of "soft Hindutva." Or, as Congress and the liberals articulate, this is "Hinduism" (a plural and tolerant narrative) versus "Hindutva" (a singular and intolerant narrative). Above all, the hard and soft Hindutva movements are anchored on apparent historical grievances or discord and seek solutions in their own ways to redress them. Therefore, it is my argument that any study of Hindu communalism or fundamentalism or nationalism in India must look at and discuss the role of individual politicians who are the manipulators of religious rhetoric.[68]

From the late nineteenth century until now, in India, "the gears of communal conflict," as William Gould also argues, are often "lubricated by competition over social and political resources, rather than the deliberate manipulation of religious symbols."[69] In this sense, I think the BJP can be labelled "Hindu nationalist," as their ideology has more to do with politics than the Hindu religion that is spiritually enriched, tolerant and very adaptable in nature. Once in office, the BJP-led government has implemented some of the traditional promises of its Hindu nationalist programme, especially rewriting history books, changing names of places deemed colonial or offensive to Hindus and banning cow slaughter. Overall, it has also involved itself in populist projects involving national unity, the fight against corruption, infrastructure development, ease of doing business and the fight against terrorism. It is also true that some leaders have damaged the spirit of Hinduism by indulging in their tirades against minorities, especially in their stance on "Hinduism" as inherently opposed to the Abrahamic religions. However, given the continuities and discrepancies of Hindu nationalism and the resistance it faces from Dalit and Muslim activists, the Hindutva movement's goal of reshaping Indian society in its own image is a far-fetched dream. Being a Hindu, I also believe in what Avijit Pathak points out as the inherent developing ethos of Hinduism:

> Its epics constantly remind me of the dharma of life, the interplay of good and evil, the dynamics of *tamas*, *rajas* and *sattwa*, and the riddle of human existence. Its Upanishads take me to the realm of sublime prayers: a longing for the transcendental – the way Rabindranath Tagore composed his enchanting songs.

Likewise, sages like Ramakrishna and Raman Maharshi arouse meditative calmness, love and ecstasy, and the likes of Vivekananda and Gandhi inspire us to unite the three yogas – love, knowledge and action. With this tradition of Hinduism, all the walls of separation are broken. Gautam Buddha and Narayan Guru, Surdas and Mira, Nizamuddin Auliya and Mother Teresa, Tagore and Nehru, and Lokayat and Vedanta: nothing is alien; it is an ocean that absorbs everything.[70]

In conclusion, the definition of India as an ocean or a space for plurality, peace and tradition is important. This space, according to Makarand R. Paranjape, offers an alternative to the Western ways and the continuation of Indian ways of thinking.[71] This should be done without demeaning Hinduism or any other religion in opposition to it. As things are still unfolding, tracing and understanding the growth of Hindu nationalism from the early days of the Hindu renaissance to the present, I do not believe that India's linguistic, cultural, religious, artistic, intellectual, social and political factors will allow any political party to shape a secular nation into a Hindu nation state.[72]

## Notes

1 I am grateful to my friend Prof. Dhananjay Singh, Chairperson of the Centre for English Studies at Jawaharlal Nehru University, for his insightful comments and timely feedback on this chapter.
2 Srinivasan, *Sweating Saris*, 63–64.
3 There is no official category called "Hindu dance" in India as such. Post-independence, the dances were collectively referred to as *Bhartiya shastriya nritya* (Indian Classical Dance). A discussion on this topic will follow in Chapter 2 of this book.
4 Lightfoot, *Lightfoot Dancing*, 2015.
5 For a detailed discussion of the idea of Hindu nationalism, see Banerjee, "'Hindutva': Ideology and Social Psychology," 1991.
6 For a detailed discussion of Hinduism's origins, its key philosophical concepts, criticism of politicised Hinduism and re-examination of Hinduism, see Tharoor, *Why I Am a Hindu*, 2018.
7 For a detailed discussion of the history of the Hindu religion and tradition, see Flood, *An Introduction to Hinduism*, 1996; Fowler, *Hinduism: Beliefs and Practices*, 1997; Lorenzen, "Who Invented Hinduism?" 1999; Klostermaier, *A Survey of Hinduism*, 2007; Whaling, *Understanding Hinduism*, 2009.
8 It is also a matter of debate whether the "Aryan invasion," as it is referred to by a school of historians, indeed took place.
9 For a discussion of Aryan invasion theory, see Parpola, *The Roots of Hinduism*, 2015; Thapar, "The Theory of Aryan Race and India," 1996.
10 Mill, *The History of British India*, 1817.
11 Sugirtharajah, *Imagining Hinduism*, ix.

12 For a detailed discussion of Hindu-Muslim polarity, see Sharma, "On Hindu, Hindustān, Hinduism and Hindutva," 2002; Thapar, "The Theory of Aryan Race and India," 1996.
13 Jones, "The Four Yugs and Ten Avatars of the Hindoos," 269.
14 Sugirtharajah, *Imagining Hinduism*, 4.
15 For a detailed discussion of the emergence and significance of the word *Hindu*, see Lorenzen, "Who Invented Hinduism?" 1999; Sharma, "On Hindu, Hindustān, Hinduism and Hindutva," 2002; See also Lochtefeld, *The Illustrated Encyclopedia of Hinduism*, ix.
16 Whaling, *Understanding Hinduism*, 14–15.
17 Brockington, *The Sacred Thread*, 24.
18 Feuerstein et al. offer seventeen arguments on why the Aryan invasion never happened. See Feuerstein et al., *In Search of the Cradle of Civilisation*, 1995.
19 Aurobindo, *The Secret of the Veda*, 553.
20 Thapar, "The Theory of Aryan Race and India," 1996.
21 Ibid., 26.
22 Thapar, "Some Appropriations of the Theory of Aryan Race Relating to the Beginnings of Indian History," 19.
23 Jackson, "The Persian Dominions in Northern India Down to the Time of Alexander's Invasion," 324–25.
24 Sharma, "On Hindu, Hindustān, Hinduism and Hindutva," 4.
25 Prabhavananda and Manchester, *The Spiritual Heritage of India*, 7, 22.
26 Ahmad, *Studies in Islamic Culture in the Indian Environment*, 77.
27 Sachau, *Alberuni's India*, 1914.
28 Ibid., 21.
29 Davis, "Introduction," 6–7.
30 Cited in Ibid.
31 Nag and Burman, *The English Works of Raja Rammohun* Roy, vol. 1, 1.
32 See Zvelebil, *The Smile of Murugan*, 1973.
33 For a discussion on Hinduism in South Indian states, see Sastry, *A History of South India*, 1955; Champakalakshmi, *Religion, Tradition, and Ideology*, 2011.
34 For a discussion of Hinduism in Kerala, see Pati, "Kerala," 2009; Menon, *A Handbook of Kerala*, 2002.
35 Jeffrey, *The Decline of Nayar Dominance*, 265.
36 Bayly, "Hindu Kingship and the Origin of Community," 178. For a discussion of political and religious system in Kerala, see also Panikkar, *A History of Kerala, 1498–1801*, 1960.
37 Ibid.
38 Ibid., 181.
39 Thapar, *Interpreting Early India*, 79. Ekanath, a popular saint of Maharashtra in the sixteenth century, said, "If I call myself a Hindu I will be beaten up, and Muslim I am not." See Joshi and Josh, *Struggle for Hegemony in India 1920–47*, 3.
40 For a discussion of the *Bhakti* movement, see Wilson, *The Religious Sects of the Hindus*, 1904; Monier-Williams, *Hinduism*, 1894; Grierson, "Bhakti-Marga," 1910.
41 For a discussion of the role of interpretation in the *Bhakti* movement, see Inden, *Imagining India*, 1992; Mishra, *Devotional Poetics and the Indian Sublime*, 1998.
42 Frykenberg, "The Emergence of Modem 'Hinduism' as a Concept and as an Institution," 31; Also see Lochtefeld, *The Illustrated Encyclopedia of Hinduism*, vii.

43 Smith, *Meaning and End of Religion*, 1963.
44 Sugirtharajah, *Imagining Hinduism*, 143.
45 Tarabout, "Malabar Gods, Nation-building and World Culture," 2005.
46 For a discussion of Swami Vivekananda's life and works, See Paranjape and Sengupta, *The Cyclonic Swami*, 2005; Paranjape, *Swami Vivekananda*, 2015.
47 For a discussion of the global appeal of Hinduism, see King, "Orientalism and the Modern Myth of 'Hinduism'," 1999; Lorenzen, "Who Invented Hinduism?" 1999.
48 For a discussion of Gandhian thought, see Paranjape, *Decolonization and Development*, 1993.
49 Gandhi, "Why I Am a Hindu," 1927.
50 Page, *Prelude to Partition*, 73–84.
51 Gould, *Hindu Nationalism and the Language of Politics in Late Colonial India*, 1.
52 The official proposal for a two-state solution to India will come in the 1940s from Muslim League leader Mohammad Ali Jinnah. Savarkar's militant Hinduism and Hindutva ideology in fuelling this solution cannot be neglected.
53 Savarkar, *Hindutva: Who Is a Hindu?* 1923/1969.
54 For a discussion on Hindutva and Hinduism, see Anderson and Damle, *The Brotherhood of Saffron*, 1987; Lipner, "On 'Hindutva' and 'Hindu-Catholic', with a Moral for Our Times," 1992; Sharma, "On Hindu, Hindustān, Hinduism and Hindutva," 2002.
55 Savarkar, *Hindutva: Who Is a Hindu?* 91.
56 Bakhle, "Country First?" 2010.
57 Banerjee, "'Hindutva': Ideology and Social Psychology," 97; See also Anderson and Damle, *The Brotherhood of Saffron*, 1987.
58 Ibid.
59 Nandy, "The Demonic and the Seductive in Religious Nationalism," 2009.
60 For a detailed discussion of Brahmabandhav Upadhyay, see Lipner, *Life and Thought of a Revolutionary*, 1999.
61 Nandy, "The Demonic and the Seductive in Religious Nationalism," 2.
62 Quoted in Nauriya, "The Savarkarist Syntax," 2014.
63 Nandy, "The Demonic and the Seductive in Religious Nationalism," 2.
64 For a detailed discussion of the glorification of Savarkar's ideology, see Basu et al., *Khaki Shorts, Saffron Flags*, 1993; Ghosh, *BJP and the Evolution of Hindu Nationalism*, 2000; Sarkar, *Beyond Nationalist Frames*, 2002; RamPrasad, "Contemporary Political Hinduism," 2003.
65 Sharma, *Hinduism*, 2015.
66 Nandy, "The Demonic and the Seductive in Religious Nationalism," 3, 6.
67 For a detailed discussion of the Hinduism of the "secular" Congress in the 1930s and 1940s, see Gould, *Hindu Nationalism and the Language of Politics in Late Colonial India*, 2004.
68 Ibid.
69 Ibid., 160. Also, look at the alliances of the "secular" Congress with Arya Samaj in late colonial India and their policy of "soft Hindutva" to defeat the Narendra Modi-led BJP in 2019.
70 Pathak, "BJP Has Insulted My Hinduism," 2019.
71 For a detailed discussion, see Paranjape, *Decolonization and Development*, 1993.
72 Doniger and Nussbaum, *Pluralism and Democracy in India*, 2015.

# 2 The Hindu dance

This chapter focusses on the idea of being Hindu and its nuances for the common people of India. Sugirtharajah writes that Hinduism, or the idea of being Hindu, "is not confined to texts or to a prescribed set of beliefs."[1] She argues that being Hindu, apart from including these aspects, "encompasses a wide variety of other areas such as art, dance, music and folklore."[2] According to the Hindu tradition and philosophy, all arts are considered to be gifts from God or are ways of accessing him. The study of Hindu dance, or Indian classical dance, portrays that this phenomenon has a long history, and it still enjoys a popular following far beyond the boundaries of India. Many scholars have noted the importance of dance in India – particularly, its importance in Hinduism. For Judith Lynne Hanna, this importance lies in dance deeply embedding in the sacred traditions of the Hindu faith.[3] This has been passed on as cultural knowledge in many communities. Noted cultural theorist Stuart Hall has also pointed to the fact that as human beings, we assign meaning through "the frameworks of interpretation which we bring to them."[4] In essence, Hindu dance explores the relationship between the primordial past of humans and the divine. Owing to its religious association with Hinduism, a dance space is not just an arena of performance but also an interpretation of the divine force.

In Hinduism, with a number of gods and goddesses, the relationship between dance and religion is intrinsic. *Nritya* (dance) is considered as the outcome of five *kriyas* (work) of God – *Avirbhava* (creation), *Isthiti* (preservation), *Samhara* (destruction), *Tirobhava* (illusion) and *Anugraha* (salvation).[5] Nataraja (Shiva) is considered as the first dancer (Figure 2.1). In the revival of Hindu dance tradition, Matthew Harp Allen argues, Nataraja became a central metaphor:

> *Nataraja*, an ancient form of the god Siva indigenous to South India, would serve as the perfect *nayaka* (lord) of the revived dance. The astonishingly beautiful bronze sculpture of Nataraja from the Cola era (ca. 9-IIth century C.E.) is today the focus of his renown in the

*Figure 2.1* Depiction of Hindu God Lord Shiva as Nataraj (God of Dance) in *Tandava*; copper alloy statue from tenth-century Chola Dynasty, Tamil Nadu, India, at the Los Angeles County Museum of Art

Photograph Courtesy: Wikimedia Commons

international art world, but even earlier (ca. 530 C.E.), *Nataraja* was depicted in stone in the Chalukya center of Badami, dancing with the wives of the rishis (sages) in the forest. As we will see, however, despite his deep roots in South Indian religious tradition, Nataraja had never before been asked to play a role quite like the one reserved for him in the 20th-century revival.[6]

Nataraja performed the vigorous cosmic dance – *tāṇḍava* – that resulted in the creation of the earth.[7] His dance form expressed an ecstasy in the creation, preservation and destruction. Gregory Bateson observes,

> Consider Shiva, the Nataraj figure, the Dancing Shiva. This is a paradigm, imposed upon the entire world of experience, in which it is assumed that everything that happens, ranging from earthquakes to gossip to murder, to joy, to love, to laughter, and all the rest, is an incredible zig-zag of what might seem otherwise to the unclassifiable and discorded experience, but is, in fact, all framed within the Shivaite concept of *The Dance*.[8]

The cosmic dance of Shiva is the manifestation of rhythms in our lives. The rhythms of the *tāṇḍava* and all such other dances were guided by the beat of the drum of Shiva. Gayanacharya Avinash C. Pandeya notes that this life is "the Centre of Universe, i.e., God within the heart."[9]

The traditional Indian dance that developed over centuries was aided by both Hindu religious and local cultural practices. Hindu temples nurtured dancers, and dances told stories from mythology.[10] According to renowned Indian dancer Shovana Narayan, most of these earlier forms of dance were largely solo and hardly any props were used by the dancers. She writes,

> Thus the onus fell on the dancer for effective communication for which they utilised "mudras" (hand gestures), "bhavas," "rasas" (moods of emotions) and expressions for enabling characters and situations to be described. Hence all dance forms were similar in their origin and ultimate aim, as they all originated as the outward manifestation of expression, borne out of deep religious sentiment.[11]

Thus, a major commonality among all the Hindu dances is the fact that they are deeply rooted in religion. Eminent dance critic and scholar Dr Sunil Kothari adds,

> Mythological and devotional stories form their content. The expressive aspect tends to revolve around a *nayika*, the heroine, who pines for union with the *nayaka*, the hero. The heroine symbolises the soul of

the devotee, and the hero, the Lord, the super-soul with whom the soul wishes to unite. The spirit of the *bhakti* movement, the cult of devotion, permeates these dance forms.[12]

Under the spirit of *bhakti* (devotion), Hindus saw dance as a means to connect or communicate with the gods.[13] This is one of the reasons that almost all Hindu dances are performed barefoot. Joan Cass in her book *The Dance* observes,

> Hindu dance is the oldest of the world's developed dance forms. Hindu dance depicts a serene and ordered universe. Gracefully intricate hand gestures and subtle facial motions tell a ritualized story from the storehouse of religious legend. There are also Hindu dances that proceed in complex rhythms whose intent is solely the offering of a prescribed pattern of motion for contemplation as a spiritual experience.[14]

The varied Indian classical dance forms that sprang from diverse traditional Hindu religious, folk or musical theatres of the past have acquired some key techniques over the years. These include – *mudras* (gestures), *rasas* (aesthetic impression) and *bhava* (mood or emotions) – mentioned in Bharata's *Natyasastra*[15] and Nandikeshwara's *Bharatarnava*. While Bharata mentions eight *rasas* – *Sringara* (Erotic), *Hasya* (Comic), *Karuna* (Pathos), *Raudra* (Furious), *Bhayanaka* (Terrible), *Vira* (Heroic), *Vibhatsa* (Disgust), and *Adbhuta* (Marvellous) – another great Sanskrit commentator Abhinaya Gupta Acharya mentions a ninth rasa (navarasas) – *Santa* (Tranquil).[16] Three classes of *bhavas* are produced with an interplay of emotions: *Sattvika* (physical), *Manasika* (action of the mind) and *Saririka* (bodily action). *Natyasastra* encompasses within itself elements of dance, drama, dialogue, and music. The four kinds of actions (*abhinayas*) – Sattvika (emotional attributes), *Angika* (body gestures), *Vacka* (vocal) and *Aharya* (dress) – are attached importance.[17] In relation to dance, the treatise mentions postures and gaits – ten *mandalas* (modes of standing), six *sthankas* (modes of resting), five *utplavanas* (kinds of leaps), seven *bhramaris* (kinds of pirouettes), thirty-two *caris* (gaits), twenty-eight *asamyukta hastas* (single hand gestures), twenty-four *samyukta hastas* (combined hand gestures) and thirty *nritta hastas* (ornate gestures).[18] The techniques mentioned in ancient Indian treatises on the performing arts have been incorporated into all the Indian classical dance forms alike.[19]

With constant invasions, especially Muslim (Mughal) and Christian (British), and an international platform, the original dance techniques were diluted to create new forms. Rita Vega de Triana observes that the wandering dancing gipsies made innovations in dance styles possible. She adds,

> It is recorded that Hindu dancers performed in the summer palace at Cadiz for the royal Spanish court, and their highly formalized gesture

language must have extended some influence on what became the "Andalucian style."[20]

In fact, the dilution and mixing are to an extent that De Triana points to similarities between Spanish Flamenco and some Hindu dances. She writes,

> As in Flamenco, the Hindu dance makes use of the hand-clap (the Spanish "palma," the Hindu "tala"). It is an essential element in timing and rhythm. The Hindi "Jhaptal" is similar to the flamenco "Bulerias" in that the hand-claps are arranged in a two-three-two-three pattern. The Indian "Chautal" is marked in steady beats of twelve, as is the flamenco "Soleares" and the "Alegrias."[21]

So, it would not be wrong to argue that Hindu religiosity was replaced by spirituality. But the basic rhythm, theme and expression remain the same.[22] Sitara Thobani notes that, in most of the Indian classical dances,

> the spiritual offers an abstract, almost universal relevance for the dance that is not dependent (at first glance) on its Hindu identification. With the origins of Indian classical dance in Hinduism already taken for granted, dancers quickly identify spirituality as the medium for their contemporary experiences in dance.[23]

Sunil Kothari observes that apart from the temples, where the dance was a part of the ritual procedures, it also existed under the patronage of royal courts in India.[24] Many institutions revolving around the figure of women dancers were common – *devadasis*, *nagar badhus*, *bhagtans* or *kalavangtis*.[25] *Devadasis* (female servants of God) were symbolically married to God and on auspicious occasions, performed at temple rituals and festivities.[26] In Hinduism, the residing deity of the temple was treated like an earthly king by people.[27] The god had a court just like the local king with ministers, musicians and dancers (*devadasis*). Local rulers often offered young girls and boys to work as musicians and *devadasis* in the temple. Soon, this became a hereditary practice, and the children of these *devadasis* continued the same profession. *Devadasis* also performed the role of courtesans, mistresses and Hindu temple workers.[28] These dancers and musicians (nattuvanar) re-enacted the mythological *Gandharvas* and *Apsaras* of heaven.[29]

The idea of *devadasis* and *nautch* girls reached Australia from Europe and the United States of America, through the discourse of imperialism (Figure 2.2). Various travel narratives, fictional texts and newspapers often delineated the details of the performances either in India or on European stages by Western dancers (white girls) impersonating oriental fantasy girls.

*Figure 2.2* Cover of *Life* magazine featuring the Baroda Nautch Girls, Bombay, India, 1936

Photograph: Vernon & Co. Photographers
Source: Gaekwads of Baroda – http://gaekwadsofbaroda.com/content/sojourn-suzerainty
Photograph Courtesy: Public Domain

## 34  The Hindu dance

In 1907, an Australian newspaper, the *Maitland Daily Mercury*, reported how the system of *nautch* girls, then popular among some rich Indians, was creating conflict in Indian society. A rich *Marwari* family (an ethnolinguistic group of Rajasthan) invited a well-known *nautch* girl of Calcutta [Kolkata], Guahar Jan, to dance and sing at a marriage ceremony in Bombay [Mumbai]. Guahar was paid Rupees 15,000 for this event and later also invited to sing at the Lady Northcote Hindu Orphanage. Hearing this, a well-known reformer and Brahmin leader of Bombay, Mr Justice Chandravarkar, resigned from the managing committee of the orphanage.

> The position of the nautch girl is no longer what it was in the Indian social system. Not merely Europeans but some of the best among the natives feel that in view of the gradual rising of the tone of society, the evils associated with her profession should cease to enjoy the toleration accorded to them in the past.[30]

Although the *nautch* girls played a significant role in the socio-cultural life of India, however, during British rule, Hindu dance forms, especially temple dancing, were looked down upon and the women performers – *devadasis* – were linked to prostitution. A former diplomat and author Pran Nevile notes,

> As the 19th century wore on, the spread of English education brought in a new petit bourgeois class which, influenced by western ideas, got alienated from the art and cultural traditions of the country. This educated group was also swayed by the writings of some foreign observers who, without understanding the origin and nature of the Indian dance art and mistaking it for a representation of erotic temple sculptures, condemned it as "repulsive and immoral."
>
> They made no distinction between an accomplished professional nautch girl or a *devadasi* and a common prostitute, dubbing both as fallen women. The educated Indians, suffering from an inferiority complex, were overcome with a sense of shame about their own traditional arts.[31]

Amrit Srinivasan in "Reform and Revival" outlines the events that led to the ban on the *devadasi* system, particularly on dedicating young girls to Hindu temples.[32] He highlights the process by which the campaign against *nautch* became linked with the politics of the Dravidian movement in South India. During the late nineteenth and early twentieth centuries, the total elimination of the *devadasi* system was demanded by reformers in the form of anti-*nautch* campaigns.[33] Nevile writes that the anti-*nautch* campaign was also supported by the Indian press and the Social Purity Associations in various parts of India, sponsored by the Purity movement in England.[34] Mahatma Gandhi, in an article published in *Young India*, described the need to put an end to the system of *devadasis* by "purifying the neighbourhood."[35] He remarks,

> Of all the addresses I received in the South, the most touching was one on behalf of the *devadasis* – a euphemism for prostitutes. It was prepared and brought by people who belong to the clan from which these unfortunate sisters are drawn . . . And let every pure man, wherever he is, do what he can to purify his neighbourhood.[36]

For Gandhi and many other Indian progressives, *devadasi* was a synonym for prostitution and an object for reform.[37] The critics of temple dancing, reformists and national leaders focussed on *devadasis* and *nautch* girls' sexual lives and presented them as victims of colonial society. In 1927, when *devadasis* protested against such portrayal, forced reforms and demanded to preserve their traditions of temple dance and service, a leading feminist Dr S. Muthulakshmi Reddy responded,

> As far as the local *devadasis'* protest, they are all set [sic] of prostitutes, who have been set up by their keepers. How can the government take cognisance of such a protest? . . . So I would request you not to pay any heed to such protests from a most objectionable class of people in the society.[38]

Pallabi Chakravorty asserts that an ironic turn of history was caused by the anti-*nautch* and *devadasis* movement. As such reform movements deemed all temple dancers to be prostitutes, in the long run, this stigmatisation forced many into actual prostitution.[39]

In the course of these ongoing debates, as a reaction to the policies of the colonial government, a revival movement started in India with an aim to create a national identity through indigenous arts. To facilitate this transformation or rescue temple dance and embody it with spiritual meaning devoid of any sensuality, *devadasis'* exclusion from the discourse of the re-creation of classical dance was necessary for reformers. This reform movement, led mostly by middle-class and upper caste men and women, saw a pressing need for the development of arts, using purified Hindu dance and devotional music. In a documentary film entitled *The Journey from Sadir to Bharatnatyam*, S. Anandhi observes, "Nationalists wanted to save dance as a pure art form and elevate it to a position of national art."[40] Cultural revivalists and Hindu activists believed that this pure or ideal art must draw on traditional Hindu idioms and should be performed by ideal women, if it were to make an impact in

India. Janaki Bakhle writes that by the end of the first decade of the twentieth century, Indian classical dance and music were taught at both homes and select schools to wives and children of the upper- and middle-class people. Dancers and musicians performed in the homes of aristocrats and elites and in public halls thus making this into a subject worthy of national attention.[41] Soon, the hereditary community of Muslim musicians and dancers in the north and the hereditary community of non-Brahmin Hindu dancers, such as *devadasis*, in the South were either disenfranchised or replaced by upper-caste Brahmin men and women dancers and musicians.[42]

Also, as part of a larger pattern of revival and promotion, in the 1930s (a volatile period for Indian culture), with the increasing awareness about Hindu dance traditions, intellectuals and artists from North, South and East India, such as Rabindranath Tagore (in Bengal), Vallathol (in Kerala), Rukmini Devi (in Chennai), Madame Menaka (in Mumbai) and Uday Shankar (in Almora) founded institutions for training in Indian dance, music and arts (Figure 2.3).[43] Their attempts were supported by frequent visits of Western dancers, such as Ragini, La Marie, Anna Pavlova and many others. These dancers asked young educated Indians to learn and promote various arts.[44] When Uday Shankar was introduced to the Devonshire audiences in the 1930s, the promoters of Dartington Hall Trust, Leonard and Dorothy Elmhirst, believed that this "new flowering of the arts could transform a society impoverished by industrialisation and secularization."[45] Paula Morel remembered his performances at that time as "magical . . . (as) though the Gods had come to Devonshire."[46] The Hindu dance and music (Bhartiya shastriya nritya and Bhartiya shastriya sangeet) were now seen simultaneously as classical and national forms that foregrounded Hindu religious beliefs.[47] Sunil Kothari points out that at most of the upcoming local dance centres and institutions, the classical Indian dances were being pursued by young women from the educated middle class. Kothari adds that although "the stigma attached to dance was not completely removed, but the change in attitude was noticeable."[48] For him, it was largely the entry of pioneering women like Rukmini Devi Arundale from the upper Brahmin class that changed the Indian classical dance scenario (Figure 2.4).[49]

Originally known as *sadir*, a dance style performed by the *devadasis*, the Indian classical dance form of Bharatanatyam owes its current name to E. Krishna Iyer and Rukmini Devi Arundale.[50] Iyer was a well-known lawyer, freedom fighter and classical arts activist. His involvement with the Bharatanatyam revival movement in South India began when he joined a theatrical company called Suguna Vilasa Sabha and learnt *sadir*. Later, he founded the Madras Music Academy to save this dance art. In 1932, at a meeting of the academy, he sought to give the *sadir* dance form a measure of respect and legitimacy by changing its name to Bharatnatyam.[51] An article titled

*Figure 2.3* Uday Shankar performing Gandharva dance, Paris, January 17, 1934
Photographer: Studio Lipnitzki
Source: www.loc.gov/item/2014649255/
Collection: *New York World-Telegram* and the *Sun* Newspaper Photograph Collection
Photograph Courtesy: Library of Congress Prints and Photographs Division Washington, D.C.

*Figure 2.4* Rukmini Devi in her 40s
Photographer: Unknown
Source: *Rukmini Devi Arundale: Birth Centenary Volume* (2003)
Photograph Courtesy: Kalakshetra Foundation

"The Renaming of an Old Dance,"[52] published by an anonymous author in *Sruti*, states,

> The reason for giving a new name to the classical dance art – of which its *devadasi* practitioners were the hereditary custodians – was the felt need to "deodorize" the dance . . . *Sadir* – and the more explicit *Dasiattam* – had acquired a bad odour because prostitution had come to be associated closely in the public's mind with the *devadasi* system. If the art had to be saved from "extinction" and given a fresh lease of life, several influential persons felt, it ought to be given a new name or identity.[53]

Rukmini Devi's intention to revive *Sadir* as Bharatanatyam was to create the temple atmosphere of the abolished dance on stage.[54] Rukmini Devi married an Australian theosophist, Dr George S. Arundale, and they saw Anna Pavlova dance in 1924 at London's Covent Garden, an experience Rukmini Devi remembered as her "first glimpse into the fairy tale world of ballet."[55] Four years later, Dr Arundale and Rukmini Devi went on a lecture tour with a theosophical entourage and met with Pavlova's troupe in Southeast Asia.[56] In 1928, the two travelled on the same ship to Australia from Surabaya and became close friends. During this time, Rukmini Devi wanted to study ballet. While sitting on the deck of the ship, Rukmini Devi said to Pavlova, "I wish I could dance like you, but I know I never can." To this, Pavlova replied, "No, no. You must never say that. You don't have to dance, for if you just walk across the stage, it will be enough. People will come to watch you do just that." Pavlova's student, Cleo Nordi, taught Rukmini Devi ballet. But it was the great ballet dancer herself who inspired Rukmini Devi to discover and revive the Indian classical dance form. Pavlova was determined to direct Rukmini Devi's interests closer to India. She told Rukmini Devi, "You CAN learn ballet but I think that everyone must try to revive the art of his own country . . . she had said the same thing to Uday Shankar who danced with her as Krishna."[57] In the mid-1930s, Rukmini Devi introduced new "symbolic phraseologies into the structure" of *sadir* and helped in its transformation into Bharatanatyam. Soon, with the inspiration and collaboration of other artists, she became a leading exponent and a reviving spirit of Bharatanatyam at her institute Kalashetra in Chennai, which brought the form to the global stage.[58]

N. Pattabhiraman observes that Rukmini Devi's unique contribution in this process of transformation of the inherited traditions of dance was "to destroy what was crude and vulgar" and "to replace them with sophistication and refined taste."[59] These dance revivalists, critics and historians used India's ancient past to re-invent "an unbroken dance tradition."[60] Avanthi

Meduri narrates a personal anecdote on how this separation of *sadir* as "impure" and Bharatanatyam as a "pure" dance form was accepted by Brahmin dance teachers and young middle-class dance students:

> My dance teachers told me a story, a story they were never tired of repeating . . . that this dance was once called *sadir* and that it was performed in the sacred precincts of the temple. They said that the *devadasi* (temple dancers) who practiced this art form lived and danced happily in the temple environments. . . . But then the *devadasi* turned "corrupt" and profaned the art form, they said suddenly, and rather angrily. Frightened by their anger, I asked rather hesitantly about how they had profaned the art. They looked around them to see if anybody was eavesdropping, and whispered into my ear: they said that dancing became associated with nautch girls because of the corrupt ways of the devadasi . . . A highly complex system rooted in religion had become "corrupted" until the "respectable" people of the south initiated a campaign in the late 1920s to abolish the ill-reputed devadasi system.[61]

According to Amrit Srinivasan, the revival movement, which was created mostly by the Brahmin leaders, hardly gave any chance to the *devadasis*. He argues that for both the reformers and the revivalists, the *devadasi* system was abhorrent because of the "institutionalization" of sexuality.[62] In this regard, Indira Viswanathan Peterson and Davesh Soneji also remark,

> The demise of *sadir* dance, and the repudiation of its aesthetic were inextricably linked with the public condemnation of the sexual morality of the devadasi and their dance. . . . Puritan colonial-nationalist ideologies of female sexuality played a central role in the criminalization of the devadasis and their dance.[63]

For arts, the traditional form of patronage was funds from princely states and wealthy patrons. The dance critic and collector of heritage items related to Indian dance Mohan Khokar, in his book *Traditions of Indian Classical Dance*,[64] observes that gradually the Indian classical dance moved away from its original form – from being controlled by temples to commercial greed.[65]

In 1947, with the introduction of the *Madras Devadasis Prevention of Dedication Act*, which later became the *Devadasi Abolition Bill*, the *devadasi* system was abolished, and women dedicated or married to God-husbands in temples were declared widows or divorcées.[66] This was also the time when classical Indian dances and institutions promoting them were firmly established. The present representations of Indian classical dance are extensions of the nationalist and postcolonial discourse.[67] The tradition of royal patronage was replaced by funding from government organisations. The Indian government, under its national and state development plans, started sponsoring bodies to promote local arts, especially classical art forms and literature. Sangeet Natak Akademi, set up in 1953, and the Sahitya Natak Akademi, set up in 1954, aimed to foster and promote the arts of music, drama and literature.[68] Various styles of Indian classical dances pointed out in this chapter, including Bharatanatyam, Kathakali, Mohiniyattam, Manipuri and Odissi, have long been associated with Hinduism.[69] Sitara Thobani argues that these dance performances were based on the modern interpretation and understanding of Hindu practices – "especially in the context of the nationalist movement that saw (and continues to see) the convergence of Hindu identity with Indian nationality."[70] During the nationalist phase, the revival of Hindu dance with an unbroken ancient tradition also came to be associated with the construction of India's secular national identity. The concept of a common heritage of all dances provided an umbrella under the term *Indian classical dance*, where various styles were put together.[71] The government of India's Ministry of Culture reorganized eleven key dance forms in a composite category called Shastriya Nritya (Indian classical dance) – Bharatanatyam, Kathakali, Kuchipudi, Manipuri, Kathak, Mohiniyattam, Odissi, Sattriya, Chhau, Gaudiya Nritya and Thang Ta – while the Sangeet Natak Akademi (The National Academy for Music, Dance and Drama) recognises only eight of these forms.[72] But even today, the apparent Hindu religious tradition, the characterisation and coding of most of these Indian classical dances is maintained for both national and international audiences. Firstly, it is done through the use of gods and goddesses, such as Shiva, Durga, Rama, Sita, Radha and Krishna, who dominate the dance performance, inscribing it within the spiritual space of the temple through invocations. Secondly, it is facilitated through the placement of the *Nataraja* (the five-faced Shiva) statue on stage. As discussed at the beginning of this chapter, Shiva is seen as the central icon of Hindu dance.

In this context, Sitara Thobani argues that by placing Shiva, the deity of dance, on the stage, audiences are reminded of the religious origins of Indian classical dance. She writes,

> Placing these deities on stage conveys to the audience the primacy of the divine over the performance, as well as to recall the supposedly longstanding history that ties together temple dance with contemporary classical dance . . . they also further assumptions of the dance as unequivocally Hindu in the most static of terms . . . the apparently Hindu characterization of the dance is maintained for audiences who are taught that the religious attributes of Indian classical dance are woven into its secular performance.[73]

## 42  The Hindu dance

The key figure in promoting *Nataraja* as the symbol of the grandeur of Hindu dance and religion was A. K. Coomaraswamy, a profound scholar of the twentieth century. His 1918 essay "The Dance of Shiva" has been the most influential publication in the remarkable popularisation of the *Nataraja* as a patron deity and new subject for the aesthetic significance of the revived dance.[74] The dance of *Nataraja* represents the cosmic activity of Shiva. He writes,

> The movement of the dancing figure is so admirably balanced that while it fills all space, it seems nevertheless to be at rest, in the sense that a spinning top or a gyrostat is at rest; thus realising the unity and simultaneity of the five activities (*Pancakrtya*, vise., production. Maintenance, Destruction, Embodiment and Release) which the symbolism specifically designates.[75]

Coomaraswamy sees *Nataraja's* dance as an interplay of the feminine *Prakriti* (nature) and the masculine *Purusha* (omnipresent spirit). He summarises his argument regarding the essential significance of the dance of Shiva thus:

> First, it is the image of his Rhythmic Play as the Source of all Movement within the Cosmos, which is Represented by the Arch: Secondly, the Purpose of his Dance is to Release the Countless souls of men from the Snare of Illusion: Thirdly the Place of the Dance, Chidambaram, the Centre of the Universe, is within the Heart.[76]

So, with the origins of Indian classical dance in Hinduism already taken for granted by the audiences, maintenance of the religious specificity in the dance performance is required through Nataraja.[77] Though, to date, there has been no agreement on who first started the practice of placing an idol of *Nataraja* on stage, Rukmini Devi was one of the first Indian dancers to do so and also to promote the practice to create the temple atmosphere on stage.[78]

The next section will discuss Kathakali, a dance form that Louise Lightfoot studied in India and promoted in Australia as inherently religious and specifically Hindu.

## Kathakali: from God's own country

Among the aforementioned Indian classical dance forms, Kathakali is considered to be one of the toughest and most highly stylised of the classical dance-drama techniques.[79] Kathakali represents an ancient form of music-theatre based in Hindu religious scriptures. According to K. Ayyappapanicker,

> Kathakali is probably the most fascinating traditional performing art form in India's rich cultural pageant . . . this uniquely interpretative dance governed by dramatic dynamics, including an elaborately defined code of body kinetics, which combines with beautifully eloquent gestural representation.[80]

The training period for Kathakali can last for eight to ten years. This long training period, which starts at the age of eleven, is essential to make the body flexible to perform rhythmic patterns and swings. Gayanacharya Avinash C. Pandeya outlines this intensive training of students under the *guru* (teacher) of a *kalari* (gymnasium):

> To achieve fluidity, a Kathakali pupil undergoes extensive and vigorous training from an early age. A complete alteration in the behaviour of the body is effected. Massages and oil baths are an essential aid to awaken muscles, joints and nerves and to control their behaviour. Each part of the body is reconditioned to call it into play at a slight actions of the actor. For a free play of emotions each *upanga* and *pratyanga* minor and accessory limb is treated separately; each finger, for instance, has an independent movement, and no two fingers move in sympathy with each other. Thus remodelled, the human body is adept to cast itself into the actions of gods and demons.[81]

Engaged in the unfolding of stories in dance or dance-drama, Kathakali originated from *Krishnanattam* (Sanskrit plays in praise of Krishna) and *Ramanattam* or *Attakatha* (Malayalam plays in praise of Rama) in the coastal state of Kerala during the seventeenth century.[82] According to Pandeya, the origins of Kathakali can actually be traced to the *tantric* (ritualistic) period of the Vedic Age.[83] It was *Ramanattam* that became very popular amongst the people of Malabar and transformed into Attakatha and finally took the shape of Kathakali.[84] In Kerala, theatrical activities embraced the world of the socio-religious life of the people. Christine Guillebaud notes that in Kerala, the performing arts are "firmly rooted in caste society and cause strong hierarchical splits in terms of religions and gender relations."[85] She highlights the following categories of plays in Kerala:

- Ritual and cult plays: *Bhagavati Pattu, Tiyattu, Panai Pattu, Kaniyar Kali, Tukku, Kaliattam* and *Daivattam*;
- Non-ritual though religious: *Cakkyar Kuttu, Krisnattam, Tattilme-Kali* and the *Ramayana* shadow play; and

- Secular plays: *Mohiniattam, Koratiattam, Kai-Kotti-Kali, Thullal-Patakam, Kol-Kali, Kalyanakkali, Kayukottikkal* and *Parisa Muttum Kali*.[86]

Incorporating several elements from other popular regional and ritualistic art forms of Kerala, Kathakali is noted chiefly for

  (i)   being an all-male domain (even female roles are played by men or adolescent boys);
 (ii)   the variety and range of characters – from noble heroes to demons;
(iii)   religious themes concerning the victory of good over evil;
 (iv)   epic stories drawn from the *Mahabharata*, the *Ramayana*, and the *Puranas*;
  (v)   attractive makeup of main characters, which can take from four to six hours of application
 (vi)   elaborate costumes, ornaments and crowns; and
(vii)   well-defined facial expressions using the eyebrows, eyeballs, cheeks, nose and chin, as well as body gestures and movements attuned to the offstage spoken narrative, music and percussion sounds (usually cymbals and a gong).[87]

On the stage, musicians stand in a half circle behind the actors. An orchestra consists of four drums (mridangam), flutes, a pair of heavy cymbals, a gong, a drum and singers. In Kathakali, the technical instruction for the representation of facial expressions that correspond to various *bhavas* or *rasas*, say *Sringara* (Erotic), is something like this:

> Open the upper lids as wide as possible. Keep the lower lids slightly closed. With the lips make a soft, relaxed smile, but do not show the teeth. Keep the gaze focused straight ahead. Having assumed this position, begin to flutter the eyebrows. Keeping the shoulders still, and using the neck, move the head first to the right, and then the left – back and forth. While keeping the external focus fixed ahead on one point, move the head to a 45-degree angle to the right, continuing to flutter the eyebrows. Repeat to the left.[88]

Characters' faces and hands reflect all the emotions in seven items that are presented in the following sequence:

  (i)   *Todayam* – the basic dance;
 (ii)   *Purappadu* – a preliminary dance that makes the debut of the hero;
(iii)   *Tiranokku* – curtain-look by evil characters and demons;

(iv) *Kummi* – preamble for the female character's appearance;
(v) *Kathakali* – the main play;
(vi) *Kalasam* – a passage of vigorous dance; and
(vii) The concluding benediction dance.[89]

Kathakali does not include any onstage dialogue at all, and, for this reason, dance critics, such as Phillip Zarrilli, have compared it, in terms of poetics and aesthetic pleasure, to the Chinese opera and Japanese *Noh*.[90] Zarrilli lists eight categories and qualities of *mudras*:

1   heroic gestures;
2   gestures for something or someone away from the body of the speaker;
3   powerful gestures;
4   gestures associated with the furious state;
5   gestures for personal relationships;
6   gestures which describe the qualities of what is seen;
7   gestures performed in the neutral and stationary position; and
8   gestures associated with the erotic and pathos in which the hands move from the left to the right as the leg is closed.[91]

Kathakali has 874 *mudras* that are listed in the *Hasthalakshana Deepika* ("Book of Hand Gestures").[92] Descriptive hand gestures are accompanied by a movement through the space to complete the meaning and follow a given pattern for the meaning to be conveyed.[93]

Manjusri Chaki-Sircar and Parbati K. Sircar suggest that for Nayar warriors, Kathakali was a reaction to foreign aggression and re-affirmation of the dominant masculine pride.[94] In the development of Kathakali, the contribution of various rulers of Kerala is enormous – personal participation, writing, maintenance of troupes, encouragement to artistes, and removing the stigma associated with the practice of this art.[95] Phillip Zarrilli notes that the "heyday" of Kathakali in Kerala occurred in the first half of the nineteenth century, under the royal patronage of Uthram Thirunal Maharaja, a connoisseur, writer and stage performer himself. After the death of Uthram in 1861, with the shifting socioeconomic order in Kerala, certain changes took place, especially among young people. Frykenberg and Tarabout remark that unlike other parts of India, like neighbouring Tamil Nadu, Hindu socio-religious reform movements appeared in Kerala only in the late nineteenth and early twentieth centuries.[96] Gradually education in English language, literature and culture grew, and people began to look down upon native art forms. Nationalist and caste-based, socio-legal reform movements arose, such as that sponsored by the Nayar Service Society.[97] Moreover, successors of Uthram at the Travancore court showed little interest in Kathakali.

All these changes resulted in a slow decline of patronage for the dance form. Alluding to this waning royal patronage, Chitra Panikkar asserts that later rulers were more interested in encouraging "Carnatic music and dances by women" and soon "disbanded" the palace *kaliyogam* (troupes) and restricted Kathakali's performances to the Sree Padmanabhaswamy Temple at Thiruvananthapuram (also known as Trivandrum). Although they felt indifferent to Kathakali, they continued with it merely because "they did not want to discontinue a tradition."[98]

Commenting on the changes taking place in Kerala and their economic impact on Kathakali, Chitra Panikkar further observes that some troupes and artists were driven "to the streets where, knowing no other profession, [they were] reduced to sheer penury."[99] In the early twentieth century, with the decline in court patronage, the disbanded artists migrated and created new troupes. These smaller troupes wandered in search of new patrons in smaller towns and villages. Although there was almost a total collapse of the feudal patronage structure, the art form still sustained itself; landlords regularly adopted troupes as status symbols, although for shorter periods of time.[100]

Gilles Tarabout observes that from the 1930s to 1950s, three different players and ideologies – Western artists, Indian nationalists and Kerala Communists – contributed in different ways and for different reasons to reforms in Malabar arts and rituals.[101] Important among these was the Indian Nationalist Movement (1890–1947), which promulgated a reaffirmation of local traditional values while focusing on some art forms as national.[102] In Kathakali's revival contributions of Maharani Sethu Parabati Bai (Queen-Mother of Travancore), Mahakavi Vallathol (Malabar's poet-laureate), Guru Kunchu Kurup and Guru Gopinath are much-admired and remembered.[103] Seeing the sad state of Kerala's cultural treasure, Mahakavi Vallathol Narayana Menon (1878–1958), a staunch nationalist, decided to protect and revive Kathakali.[104] Poet Vallathol, with the help of Mukund Raja, decided to use the system of *gurukulam* (residential school) along with a new management method based on the model of ballet companies, and to this end, he started Kerala Kalamandalam on land gifted by the government of Kochi on the banks of the River Bharathappuzha on the Malabar Coast of Kerala.

In fact, the revival of Kathakali, and its acceptance as a recognizable part of the Indian national performing arts tradition, parallels that of Bharatanatyam achieved by Rukmini Devi at Kalashetra in Chennai in the first half of the twentieth century.[105] Pandeya notes that it is because of the efforts of Vallathol and his troupe of dancers that the magnificent dance-art of Kathakali was able to receive popular appreciation. Predicting the future of Kathakali in India and on the international stage, he writes,

> The modernisation of Kathakali, or its adaptation to the changes in the outlook of the people especially of Kerala has secured for it great

recognition from art connoisseurs, who, having found in it a treasure house of histrionic art, have made a statement, needing no qualification, that the art of Kathakali will never die so long as ancient Hindu traditions, culture and civilization, and creative art survive in earth.[106]

The sole purpose of Kerala Kalamandalam was to revive the art form, provide support to artist-teachers and train new students without depending on one person's or a wealthy house's patronage. In the 1920s, this institute ran as a registered society and faced a shortage of funds. But it also attracted the best artists; hence, Poet Vallathol organised fundraising shows all over India and Ceylon (renamed Sri Lanka in 1972) to renovate and strengthen Kalamandalam. In 1941, the institute was taken over by the government of Kochi, but Vallathol remained its president and artistic director.[107] Kathakali artists trained at Kalamandalam, such as Ananda Shivaram, Chathunni Panicker and Kalamandalam Gopi (born Govindan Nair), realising that they could not depend on government funding and local shows or patronage anymore, started looking for new audiences, connoisseurs and impresarios outside India and Ceylon. In the 1960s, the International Centre for Kathakali was established in New Delhi. The purpose of this institute was to "lift Kerala's Kathakali from its regional character, and to import it to a new dimension by making this unique art known to audiences drawn from not only the various States of India but also from other countries."[108] This meant that Kathakali, known for its strict codes and conventions, was ready for adaptation, experimentation and change.

In the nineteenth and twentieth centuries, colonialism, orientalism and nationalism came together in various combinations to make this traditional South Indian performing art a global art form.[109] Dance and other artistic practices have greatly attracted the attention of the political elites in Kerala and thus helped in developing a broad cultural policy, promoting local traditional heritage in tandem with the nationalist project for preserving and spreading the Indian cultural tradition.[110] Satish Deshpande notes that the post-independence period in India was a time when "development" as an ideology was trying to ensure the mutual coherence of "political legitimacy, cultural identity and class relations."[111] Pandit Jawaharlal Nehru, the first prime minister of India, addressing a group of Gond dancers in 1955, observed that artists should think of themselves and their arts as Indian:[112]

> I have seen your folk dances . . . and I have found them quite enchanting. . . . You should not think that you have to [give up] your songs and dances. They are not bad. . . . You have to bear one thing in your mind that whether you reside here in Bastar or at Delhi or in any other part of the country, we are all sailing in the same ship in the sea. . . . Therefore

48  *The Hindu dance*

we all have to do our jobs in close cooperation and to forge ourselves and our country ahead to achieve progress and prosperity.[113]

The Nehruvian ideal of national unity in cultural diversity meant representing the different folk traditions of the various Indian states as an Indian aesthetic that appealed to the national sensibility of the audiences and created a sense of harmony (Figure 2.5).[114] This is problematic. As an emphasis on the common obligation to build the nation underlines how such artists and dance forms become symbols of a sense of pride in Indian nationhood. Within this context, Kathakali has been marketed by many agents for diverse reasons – promotion of Hindu traditional dance, Indian classical dance and Kerala art. Also, among all the traditional Hindu or Indian classical dance forms, it has received the greatest attention on the global stage, predominantly through the performances of Ananda Shivaram and his Australian impresario, Louise Lightfoot. The subtle expressions of a performer's face, the very slow movements of the body, the elaborate costumes and makeup, and the refined

*Figure 2.5* Mahatma Gandhi with Pandit Jawaharlal Nehru and Khan Abdul Ghaffar Khan at the Asian Relations Conference in New Delhi, April, 1948

Photograph: Press Information Bureau, Government of India
Collection: Gandhi Photos, 1886–1948
Source: https://digicoll.manoa.hawaii.edu
Photograph Courtesy: University of Hawaii

process of acting, along with experimental changes that have modernised this Indian form, have enabled it to gain recognition worldwide.[115]

It is with this background and amongst such turmoil – the Indian national movement and independence, the rise of Hindutva and Hindi nationalism (nijbhasa versus rashtrabhasha), the growing concept of a common Indian heritage and support or lack of support from the Indian government for some dance forms – that Anada Shivaram thought of taking Kathakali dance out of India onto a global cultural stage. He had seen the success of the great Uday Shankar and Ram Gopal. Recognising the importance of marketing and collaboration with a Western impresario, he agreed to create experimental hybridisation of dance productions to the extent where a positive cross-cultural exchange could take place without undermining his own talent or the sacred nature of the Hindu dance.

### Notes

1 Sugirtharajah, *Imagining Hinduism*, 140.
2 Ibid.
3 Hanna, *Dance, Sex, and Gender*, 97.
4 Hall, *Representation*, 3.
5 Pandeya, *The Art of Kathakali*, 1.
6 Allen, "Rewriting the Script for South Indian Dance," 64.
7 For a detailed discussion of various forms of *tāṇḍava*, see Chandra, *Encyclopaedia of Hindu Gods and Goddesses*, 121; Coomaraswamy, *The Dance of Shiva*, 1975.
8 Bateson, "Play and Paradigm," 14.
9 Pandeya, *The Art of Kathakali*, xi.
10 Wendy Doniger O'Flaherty writes, "Every Hindu myth is different; all Hindu myths are alike. In spite of the deep-seated, totally compelling world-view that moulds every image and symbol, every word and idea of any Hindu myth, in spite of the stress placed upon traditional form at the expense of the individual artist, each myth celebrates the belief that the universe is boundlessly various, that everything occurs simultaneously, that all possibilities may exist without excluding each other." For a detailed discussion, see O'Flaherty, *Hindu Myths*, 11.
11 Narayan, *The Sterling Book of Indian Classical Dances*, 10.
12 Kothari, "New Directions in Indian Dance: An Overview 1980–2006," 2008.
13 Narayan, *The Sterling Book of Indian Classical Dances*, 9.
14 Cass, *The Dance*, 28.
15 Often referred to as the fifth *veda* in Hinduism.
16 Pandeya, *The Art of Kathakali*, 95.
17 Ibid., 4.
18 Narayan, *The Sterling Book of Indian Classical Dances*, 12.
19 Bharata's *Natyasastra*, written during the period between 200 BCE and 200 CE, is considered the fifth *veda* (Sanskrit scripture). Containing 6,000 *slokas/sutras* (verse stanzas) on the theory of *bhavas* (feelings) and *rasas* used in classical performing arts (theatre, dance, and music), it has had a key influence on

50    The Hindu dance

      classical playwrights and dancers. According to this treatise, God Brahma, the Creator of the World, invented the art and science of classical dancing and then taught it to the most reverend sage Bharata, who passed on this art to divine beings and humans to enlighten them. Other Indian art dance forms yet to be recognised as classical dance are *Andhra Natyam*, *Vilasini Nrityam/Natyam*, and *Kerala Natanam*.
20 De Triana, *Antonio Triana and the Spanish Dance*, 94.
21 Ibid.
22 Ibid.
23 Thobani, *Indian Classical Dance and the Making of Postcolonial National Identities*, 2017.
24 Kothari, "New Directions in Indian Dance: An Overview 1980–2006," 2008.
25 Narayan, *The Sterling Book of Indian Classical Dances*, 17.
26 Davesh Soneji provides a comprehensive historical portrait of devadasis and the social reform in the South Indian community that led to the demise of this system, see Soneji, *Unfinished Gestures*, 2012.
27 Kersenboom-Story, *Nityasumangali: Devadasi Tradition in South India*, 1987.
28 Soneji, *Unfinished Gestures*, 3.
29 Pandeya, *The Art of Kathakali*, 16.
30 "The Nautch Girl," 1907.
31 Nevile, "Echoes of a Lost Tradition," 1996.
32 Srinivasan, "Reform and Revival: The Devadasi and Her Dance," 1985; see also Kersenboom-Story, *Nityasumangali: Devadasi Tradition in South India*, 1987.
33 Anandhi, "Representing Devadasis," 746.
34 Nevile, "Echoes of a Lost Tradition," 1996; See also Hubel, "The High Cost of Dancing," 2005.
35 Gandhi, *To the Women*, 166–67.
36 Ibid.
37 Anandhi, "Representing Devadasis," 741.
38 Quoted in Ibid.
39 Chakravorty, *Bells of Change*, 2008.
40 Chauhan, *The Journey from Sadir to Bharatanatyam*, 2015.
41 Bakhle, *Two Men and Music*, 2005.
42 Allen, "Rewriting the Script for South Indian Dance," 65; Qureshi, "Whose Music?" 1991.
43 Kothari, "New Directions in Indian Dance," 2008; Purkayastha, "Dancing Otherness," 2012.
44 Pandeya, *The Art of Kathakali*, xii.
45 Young, *The Elmhirsts of Dartington*, 100.
46 Khokar, *His Dance, His Life*, 91; see also Vertinsky and Ramachandran, "Uday Shankar and the Dartington Hall Trust," 2018.
47 Bakhle, *Two Men and Music*, 2005.
48 Kothari, "New Directions in Indian Dance," 2008.
49 Kothari, *Bharata Natyam*, 166–67.
50 Weidman, *Singing the Classical, Voicing the Modern*, 2006.
51 Ibid.
52 Arudra, "The Renaming of an Old Dance," 30–31.
53 Ibid.
54 Ramnarayan, "Rukmini Devi: Dancer and Reformer, a Profile," 29.
55 Ramnarayan, "Rukmini Devi: A Quest for Beauty, a Profile," 28.

56 Theosophy, derived from the Greek word *theosophia*, means divine wisdom. Its main aim is to impart teachings on the subject of integral knowledge of the state of human consciousness, universe, humanity, and divinity. The Theosophical Society was founded in 1875 by Helena Petrovna Blavatsky with Colonel Henry Steel Olcott and others in New York, USA. Its international headquarters is at Adyar in Chennai, India, and it has been in existence in Australia since 1895. For a detailed discussion, see Roe, *Beyond Belief*, 1986.
57 Ramnarayan, "Rukmini Devi: A Quest for Beauty, a Profile," 28–29.
58 In 1966, she toured Australia with her Indian Dance Company and school (Kalashetra) and participated in the Perth Festival. See also O'Shea, *At Home in the World*, 2007; Bilimoria, "Traditions and Transition in South Asian Performing Arts in Multicultural Australia," 116; Bilimoria, "Indian Dance," 330; Bapat, *Re-scribing Tradition*, 55; Venkataraman, *Indian Classical Dance*, 2015.
59 Pattabhiraman, "The Trinity of Bharatanatyam," 24.
60 Chakravorty, "From Interculturalism to Historicism," 113.
61 Meduri, "Bharatha Natyam," 1.
62 See Srinivasan, "Reform and Revival: The Devadasi and Her Dance," 1985; Srinivasan, "Temple 'Prostitution' and Community Reform," 1984.
63 Peterson and Soneji, *Performing Pasts*, 18.
64 Khokar, *Traditions of Indian Classical Dance*, 1979.
65 Purie, "Dance Forms," Book Review, 1979.
66 See also Srinivasan, *Sweating Saris*, 151; Hubel, "The High Cost of Dancing," 2005; Soneji, *Unfinished Gestures*, 2012.
67 See also Chakravorty, "From Interculturalism to Historicism," 108.
68 Katrak, *Contemporary Indian Dance*, 36.
69 Meduri, "Labels, Histories, Politics," 2008a; Allen, "Rewriting the Script for South Indian Dance," 1997; Kothari, *Bharata Natyam*, 2007.
70 Thobani, *Indian Classical Dance and the Making of Postcolonial National Identities*, 147.
71 Chakravorty, "From Interculturalism to Historicism," 111.
72 For a discussion of the development of Indian dance forms, see Bose, "The Evolution of Classical Indian Dance Literature," 1989.
73 Thobani, *Indian Classical Dance and the Making of Postcolonial National Identities*, 153.
74 Coomaraswamy, *The Dance of Shiva*, 1975.
75 Coomaraswamy, *History of Indian and Indonesian Art*, 127.
76 Coomaraswamy, *The Dance of Shiva*, 77.
77 Thobani, *Indian Classical Dance and the Making of Postcolonial National Identities*, 157.
78 See Allen, "Rewriting the Script for South Indian Dance," 79; Ramnarayan, "Rukmini Devi: Dancer and Reformer, a Profile," 29.
79 For a detailed history of Kathakali, see Bapat, *Re-scribing Tradition*, 55–82.
80 Ayyappapanicker, *Kathakali: The Art of the Non-worldly*, 1993.
81 Pandeya, *The Art of Kathakali*, 54.
82 Raghavan, *Folk Plays and Dances of Kerala*, 1947.
83 Pandeya, *The Art of Kathakali*, 34.
84 A local variant known as the *Wayang-Organ* of Java is inspired by Kathakali. See Ibid., 46.
85 Guillebaud, "Music and Politics in Kerala," 51.
86 Ibid., 23.

52  The Hindu dance

87 The male-oriented nature of Kathakali can be contrasted with Mohiniyattam, performed solely by women in Kerala. While Kathakali represents the heroic, Mohiniyattam puts a strong emphasis on the expression of grace and erotic emotions. See Bapat, *Re-scribing Tradition*, 55; Srinivasan, *Sweating Saris*, 62–63.
88 Zarrilli, *Kathakali Dance Drama*, 79.
89 Pandeya, *The Art of Kathakali*, 50.
90 Zarrilli, *Kathakali Dance Drama*, 39.
91 Ibid., 77.
92 Venu, *The Language of Kathakali*, 2000.
93 Fischer-Lichte, *Dionysus Resurrected*, 192.
94 Chaki-Sircar and Sircar, "Indian Dance," 147–64.
95 Pandeya, *The Art of Kathakali*, 40.
96 See Frykenberg, "The Emergence of Modem 'Hinduism' as a Concept and as an Institution," 1989; Tarabout, "Malabar Gods, Nation-building and World Culture," 191.
97 Also known as the Nair Service Society, it was established in 1914 by Mannathu Padmanabha Pillai for the social advancement and welfare of the Nair community. The Nairs or Nayars were historically a military caste, but a confrontation with British colonial forces in 1808–1809 led the British to limit Nair participation in combat. After the Travancore War, the Raja kept only some Nair battalions in a police capacity, dismissing the others. Some of these warriors displaced from the field of battle became well entrenched in the art of *Kathakali* and showcased their martial skills and male ethos symbolically onstage. This also explains why emotions like *vira* (heroic) and *raudra* (furious) dominate *Kathakali* performances. See Panikkar, *A History of Kerala, 1498–1801*, 1960; Ramachandran, *Empire's First Soldiers*, 2008.
98 Panikkar, "Patrons, Troupes, and Performers," 38.
99 Ibid.
100 Ibid. See also Zarrilli, *Kathakali Dance Drama*, 29; Bapat, *Re-scribing Tradition*, 64.
101 The Communist party in Kerala grew a base amongst the intellectuals and writers in Kerala. Tarabout, "Malabar Gods, Nation-building and World Culture," 193.
102 See Shah, "State Patronage in India," 126, 130.
103 Pandeya, *The Art of Kathakali*, 162.
104 Vallathol, along with Kumaran Asan and Ulloor S. Parameswara Iyer, was one of the triumvirate poets of modern Malayalam language. A great admirer of Mahatma Gandhi, Vallathol was also a nationalist poet, who wrote a series of poems on the Indian freedom movement and Communist ideology and against caste restriction, feudal tyrannies, and sociocultural orthodoxies.
105 See Srinivasan, *Sweating Saris*, 144; O'Shea, *At Home in the World*, 2007; Bilimoria, "Traditions and Transition in South Asian Performing Arts in Multicultural Australia," 116; Bilimoria, "Indian Dance," 330; Bapat, *Re-scribing Tradition*, 55; Venkataraman, *Indian Classical Dance*, 2015.
106 Pandeya, *The Art of Kathakali*, 169.
107 In the mid-1950s, the prime minister of India, Pandit Jawaharlal Nehru, provided some funding to the institute. In 2006, after periods of uncertainty under government administration, the University Grants Commission (UGC)

accorded Kerala Kalamandalam the status of Deemed University for Art and Culture.
108 International Centre for Kathakali 1968 New Delhi program, cited in Zarrilli, *Kathakali Dance Drama*, 179.
109 Peterson and Soneji, *Performing Pasts*, 1–3; Younger, *Playing Host to the Deity*, 2002.
110 Guillebaud, "Music and Politics in Kerala," 29.
111 Deshpande, "From Development to Globalization," 99.
112 The Gond are an Adivasi or scheduled tribe spread over the states of Madhya Pradesh, Maharashtra, Chhattisgarh, Uttar Pradesh, Telangana, Andhra Pradesh, Bihar and Orissa.
113 Cited in Ashley, "Recodings," 269–70.
114 See also Jain, "India's Republic Day Parade, Restoring Identities, Constructing the Nation," 2002; Fischer-Lichte, *Dionysus Resurrected*, 2013.
115 See Bapat, *Re-scribing Tradition*, 55.

# 3 The Australian mother of Kathakali[1]

Louise Lightfoot (a.k.a. Louisa Mary Lightfoot), born in Yangery (near Warrnambool, Victoria) on 22 May 1902, was the fourth child and third daughter of Victorian-born parents, Charles Lightfoot, a schoolteacher, and his wife Mary, née Graham.[2] Mary Louise Lightfoot notes,

> Louise Lightfoot was born into a line of strong, independent women and a family of teachers. All four of her grandparents were pioneers who had travelled separately from England and Ireland then met and married their life partners in Australia.[3]

At the Catholic Ladies' College, East Melbourne, she won exhibitions in drawing and mathematics, and in 1920, her father sent her to study architecture at the University of Melbourne.[4] She passed her final subjects in the Diploma of Architecture in 1925, the first woman to have then done so.[5] While still a student, she began a four-year apprenticeship in the innovative architectural office of Walter Burley Griffin and Marion Mahony Griffin in Melbourne (Figure 3.1).[6] Louise remarks that although the Griffin's did not take apprentices, the famous architects made an exception:

> I arrived at the door of (Griffin's) Melbourne office wearing a helio blouse and a grey costume – two colours I was afterwards to hear described (by Marion) as not "colours at all." One of the juniors, I considered myself the dunce in the Melbourne office and scarcely dared speak to such mature architects as Roy Lippincott and Edward Fielder Bilson, though felt quite at home with the brilliant young Henry Pynor and others.[7]

In 1925, the Griffins moved to Castlecrag, Sydney, a new suburb intended as an ideal community in harmony with nature and culture.[8] Louise went

*Figure 3.1* Walter Burley Griffin and Marion Griffin in their garden at Castlecrag with architect Louise Lightfoot and Walter's father, George Griffin, 1927
Photograph: Herbert
Source: http://nla.gov.au/nla.obj-150279355. Call No. PIC/9929/3007 LOC ALBUM 1092/19
Photograph Courtesy: National Library of Australia, Canberra

too but a bit dismayed as a mate to Marion and as a planner and designer for Griffin's office.

> Imagine my dismay when, as a young woman of 23 years, I received a request from my "boss" Walter Burley Griffin to leave Melbourne and go to Sydney as a companion and assistant to his wife Marion. She was living and drafting on her own at Castlecrag, the safeguarded foreshore suburb-to-be, which was Mr Griffin's inspired plan for Middle Harbour, Sydney.
> What a shock to have to leave my home and parents for the first time, and also to leave the office in Melbourne where I had worked happily with the other young draftsmen and with my girl-friend Cappy the typist.[9]

Louise could have said no to the Griffins but went on to this new adventure anyway. In the words of Walter Griffin, Louise showed "resourcefulness and trustworthiness, as well as artistic comprehension and diligence."[10]

Marion liked Louise, as their interests aligned in artistic activities. Louise, who was "tall, slender and graceful, striking in profile, beautiful rather than pretty," enjoyed dancing but could see no way to practise it as a profession.[11]

> I was crazy about dancing. Dancing at Carlyons, the Palais, hostess dances at Melba Hall and at the Beach Palais at Mornington! My boyfriends were recruited for dance-partners. My brother George, an excellent dancer, saw to it that I was never a wallflower.[12]

Louise found Marion "outspoken and passionate"[13] and observed,

> She was a remarkable woman, her husband's devoted and capable executrix and the supervisor of his young draftsmen. She was my instructress, and I still hear the sound of her ring scratching the paper as she rubbed out the mistakes in my drawing. "Keep your mind open to the inspiration of the Creator," she would advise, "and then I will come and pick it to pieces."[14]

Marion knew that Louise was fond of dancing and encouraged her natural talent and love for dance. Louise started learning "Eurhythmic" Greek dancing from Gertrude Sievers and found it "a little dull." On Anna Pavlova's first tour of Australia, in 1926, Louise found her fusion of classical technique and romantic emotion a "revelation."[15] She wrote,

> The greatest and perhaps the most influential event in my life was the coming of the Pavlova Company to Sydney. I sat in the gallery of a Sydney theatre watching Pavlova in the ballet Giselle. She entered crossing the stage with a lily in her arms, and I was aware for a fraction of a second that I was in a sphere millions of miles above in a state of perfection.[16]

Louise attended Pavlova's all-ballet presentations, and inspired by seeing Pavlova dance Grand Russian ballet, she dreamed of bringing the same to life in Australia (Figure 3.2).[17]

Through the Griffins, she met the Russian folk dancer Misha Burlakov, who had danced with Pavlova's tour.[18] Louise persuaded him to teach her the Russian *mazurka* and felt that her "real happiness started" when she danced with him in "peasant costume and red leather boots."[19] The "tall, willowy blonde" (Lightfoot) and the "strong, dark, jolly Russian" (Burlakov) danced

*Figure 3.2* Anna Pavlova in *Oriental Impressions* (1923)
Photograph: Nicolas Yarovoff, Montevideo
Source: http://nla.gov.au/nla.obj-141363897. Call No. PIC P348/AP/29 LOC ALBUM 810/4
Photograph Courtesy: National Library of Australia, Canberra

at clubs, parties and soirees in the homes of artistic or wealthy Sydneysiders.[20] Marion Griffin, in her memoir *Magic of America*, notes how Louise and Misha made her Castlecrag soirees lively:

> From now on Louie [Louise] was taking the dance seriously. . . . With the dance, Castlecrag came alive, a truly live spot in Australia, and always more and more alive though only a handful of people in the early days . . .
>
> At our wonderful Castlecrag parties, the finest musical talent and many visiting artists came and sang and played for us. The young folk [including Louie and Cappy] arranged delightful programs. I always left the arrangements of the parties entirely in their hands. The ballet was inaugurated – Louie went ahead with enthusiasm and industry, even with the surprising feats that Russians do.[21]

The duo studied whatever forms of dance they could find and opened a dance school (Castlecrag Dancing School) teaching folk dances, also known as "character" dance and ballet, to a growing number of students. Louise took tuition from Ivan Sergieff, who was a member of Pavlova's dance company in both Australian tours. It is around this time that Louise wanted to end her relations with Marion. Mary Louise Lightfoot suggests that Louise was in a relationship with Misha. In Louise's own words, Marion objected to this affair:

> Marion was objecting to my continued companionship with Misha after the arrival of his wife and children in Sydney. But I was determined to go my own way and by now more than ever longed to have a dance career, with Misha as my willing helper.[22]

Soon, Louise and Misha established a ballet studio and large dance school at Circular Quay, Sydney, out of which would grow the First Australian Ballet.[23] The first public appearances by the dancers of the Lightfoot-Burlakov school were in 1929, when Louise and Misha, along with some of their pupils, began appearing in opera performances, dance recitals and various divertissements (Figure 3.3).[24] Louise's passion for dance was the driving force, complemented by Misha's dancing, mime and carpentry skills. They took every opportunity to "show their girls" on stage, and the students helped with costumes and scenery. At the request of the Feminist Club and the Theosophical Society,[25] they performed in pageants and revues, at fetes and garden parties, in aid of Music Week, the Red Cross or the Women's Hospital; the students and parents "contributed culturally and financially while building their repertoire of dances and excerpts."[26] In 1930, Louise studied modern dance with Sonia Revid, in the technique of Mary Wigman, and added to their repertoire dances in that starkly modern style.[27]

*The Australian mother of Kathakali* 59

*Figure 3.3* (Left to Right) Louise Lightfoot and Misha Burlakov in *Dance Brutale*
Photographer: Unknown
Source: Photograph from the Louise Lightfoot Bequest, Monash University
Photograph Courtesy: Music Archives of Monash University and Mary Louise Lightfoot

By March 1931, these early initiatives had developed to the stage, and they were able to present their first classical dance production. Mary Louise Lightfoot notes that Rukmini Arundale, who had settled for some time in Sydney, stimulated the idea of a larger stage production for Lightfoot and Burlakov's students in which she would dance in Pavlova's own creation *Indian Wedding* (along with *The Heart of Russia*). This was seen as part of *Oriental Impressions*, a ballet created from Uday Shankar's collaboration with Pavlova (Figure 3.4).[28] As noted in Chapter 2, Rukmini Devi had met Pavlova on the ship to Australia. She had also been studying ballet for some time at the Lightfoot-Burlakov studio. Her marriage at the young age of sixteen to Dr George Arundale, enabled Rukmini Devi to travel extensively and see a variety of artistic traditions (Figure 3.5). Carl Sauer conducted the orchestra while Julian Ashton supervised

*Figure 3.4* Uday Shankar and Anna Pavlova in *Krishna and Radha*, ca. 1922
Photographer: Unknown
Source: *Uday Shankar* (RIMPA and the Uday Shankar Festival '83 Committee, 1983)
Photograph Courtesy: Dr Sunil Kothari and Indira Gandhi National Centre for the Arts

*The Australian mother of Kathakali* 61

*Figure 3.5* Bishop (Dr) George Arundale with his wife, Rukmini Devi Arundale, New South Wales, February 24, 1926

Photograph: *Sydney Mail* (Fairfax Corporation)
Source: http://nla.gov.au/nla.obj-162454055. Call No. PIC/15611/11955 LOC Cold store PIC/15611 Fairfax archive of glass plate negatives
Photograph Courtesy: National Library of Australia, Canberra

the décor and production of the Lightfoot-Burlakov creation. This performance at the Savoy Theatre, Sydney, was the birth of the First Australian Ballet, a non-professional group, composed of amateur dancers.[29]

In November 1931, the First Australian Ballet presented their first full ballet production – a two-act version of *Coppelia* (Figure 3.6).[30] In J. C. Williamson's library, Lightfoot found a score of this ballet with extensive notes.[31] Burlakov had seen Geneé's version, and Louise was confident that she could design, produce and stage it. On November 4, 1931, at the Savoy Theatre, Sydney, Burlakov danced as Franz, and the role of Swanhilda was shared between Jessie Cree (Act I) and Bertha Minoutochka (Act II). Louise wrote in the program notes of the performance,

> The love and adaptability for the dance in Australians, their exceptional sense of rhythm, the vitality and energy of a healthy nation, the talent

*Figure 3.6* Poster of *Coppelia* featuring Louise Lightfoot and Misha Burlakov, 1931
Photographer: Unknown
Source: Photograph from the Louise Lightfoot Bequest, Monash University
Photograph Courtesy: Music Archives of Monash University and Mary Louise Lightfoot

of individual dancers makes it the right place for the new First Australian Ballet.[32]

Her task was difficult but full of patriotism for Australia and a passion for art. Dance critic Valerie Lawson called the First Australian Ballet "the starting block of professional ballet in Australia" and "an important building block for the professional companies to follow."[33] Mary Louise Lightfoot notes that the success of *Coppelia* soon prompted the art and ballet lovers of Sydney to request repeat performances.

> A new appreciation of classical dance began to blossom in Sydney. Soon there were hundreds of requests for a repeat performance of *Coppelia*, and many new students enrolled at the school. A cutting in a scrapbook reported that Professor (later Sir) Bernard Heinz, the orchestral conductor, was greatly interested and wished to direct an orchestra for some future ballets.[34]

The company continued to perform regularly either in theatres or on stages in the studio, at get-togethers or monthly meetings and at fundraisers over the next decade. The Lightfoot-Burlakov studio also became a meeting place for visiting artists and dancers. Some of the main dancers and performers at these meetings were Moya Beaver, Trafford Whitelock, Bette Ainsworth, Gwen Ainsworth, Dorothy Evans and Sylvia Evans. Peter Finch, Ronnie Randell and John Antill attended classes at the Lightfoot-Burlakov studio and appeared in a few productions.[35] This was the time when Louise completely involved herself in teaching, ballet production, choreography, fundraising performances and financial management of the school (Figure 3.7). In 1936, Louise choreographed her version of *Petrouchka*.[36] This production featured Trafford Whitelock as Petrouchka, Moya Beaver as the ballerina and Misha Burlakov as the Blackamoor. It was presented, in July 18–20, 1936, at the Conservatorium, Sydney. Other works presented by the company in the 1930s included *Le Carnaval, Walpurgis Night, Les Sylphides, Le Spectre de la Rose, Scheherazade* and *Roksanda* (with a commissioned score from Roy Maling).[37]

Louise choreographed and produced several ballets a year in the 1930s, sometimes from her memory of productions seen in Australia and often from descriptions in books and magazines. According to Moya Beaver, a former student of the Lightfoot-Burlakov School and a principal dancer of the First Australian Ballet company,

> Louise was a brilliant choreographer. She would only have to listen to music to know what dance movements should go with it. She also seemed to know instinctively which students were suitable for which parts.[38]

Lightfoot-Burlakov faced many difficulties in producing their works – ranging from studios in buildings which were threatened to be pulled down to getting copyrights of musical scores and performance rights from overseas

*Figure 3.7* Poster of *Walpurgis Night* and *Les Sylphides* featuring Louise Lightfoot and Misha Burlakov, 1932

Photograph Courtesy: Music Archives of Monash University and Mary Louise Lightfoot

publishers and companies.[39] Mary Louise Lightfoot observes that Louise was an exceptional teacher and would go to any lengths to inspire her students:

> Louise would manifest the educational and teaching background of her family in unusual ways throughout her life. She realised the great pool of talent in young people, inspired and promoted the appreciation of and active participation in the arts, especially dancing, in thousands of young people. She was a good teacher, a perfectionist, and would train dancers for the rest of her life.[40]

So, in 1937, to learn more about emerging dance styles and see performances of various ballet productions and to secure the rights to perform a number of new ballets, Louise visited London and Paris with Misha. Mary Louise Lightfoot notes that the nineteen-year-old Moya Beaver was almost pressured by Louise to take charge of the dance school in her absence. Moya reluctantly accepted the charge, and her father made sure that it was done legally with a proper legal contract and not just based on trust.[41] When the ship stopped in Bombay en route, Louise straightaway "fell under the spell of India."[42] She "purchased Indian dance costumes and socialised with handsome Indians back on board, almost to the displeasure of the mostly white passengers."[43] Louise noted about her experience,

> A very strange thing happened to me when we neared the shore of India and were standing on the deck watching the figures on the wharf grow more distinct . . . I had never had any special interest in India. My heart was set on Europe . . . I was amazed then at this great flood of ecstasy which now came over me – ecstasy, anticipation, reverence, yearning, a bursting sensation as if my whole body would dissolve. I remember as we walked the streets of Bombay that day, I had the feeling of being "home at last."[44]

In Paris, the new home of Russian ballet, Louise and Misha found the coveted ballet scores and Louise also attended classes with famous Russian émigré teachers and experts in modern, Spanish and Hindu dances.[45] She wrote a letter to Moya Beaver, then a principal dancer and in charge of the First Australian Ballet company's studio/school, explaining why Paris is the artistic capital of the world:

> We began visiting the famous schools this week. I have learnt two Spanish routines from Nina Krisanova, one routine from Nyota Inyoka (Hindoo) [sic] and am having ballet lessons from Egorova. Private

> lessons are fiercely expensive (30 shillings a lesson, though class lessons are reasonable at 3 shillings or 12.50 francs). We saw Maurice Chevalier in the flesh at the Casino. He's a darling! Misha also met Ivan Sergieff who we studied with during his visits to Australia with Pavlova's company.[46]

She further writes,

> Almost every night we attended Ballet at the Grand Opera Comique, where I took notes on ballet which I thought suitable for our own productions. Naturally, we had to see famous churches, galleries and gardens, to say nothing of Follies Bergere, Café Hungaria, etc. Often I was extremely exhausted.[47]

In her letter to Moya, she shares her feelings thus: "My mind was constantly going back to India, and I would have been run down many a time by dense traffic had it not been that Misha looked after me."[48] Louise was particularly impressed by seeing Indian dance for the first time – performances by the great Indian dancer and impresario Uday Shankar and his Indian Dance Company. In one of her letters to students in Sydney, Louise writes,

> One fine day a poster, printed in violet ink, appeared on Paris hoardings advertising. "UDAY SHANKAR ET SA COMPAGNIE DE DANSEUSES, DANSEURS ET MUSICIANS HINDOUS." Imagine my excitement! Ballet lessons were promptly "cut," and I immediately went to the particular theatre to find out more about this forthcoming event – Shankar was to give a season from the fourteenth to the twentieth of June at the Comedie des Theatre Champs Elysees. Now the greatest excitement of all – a ballet from India![49]

After seeing the show, Louise waited outside the dressing rooms to see Uday Shankar. Finally, she got a chance to meet the world-renowned artist himself. She says:

> Later, at my interview with this handsome Indian, I requested some lessons in Kathakali. He made a statement that I doubted at the time, but since learnt was true.
> "I really know very little about Indian dancing," he said. "I must myself go back to India and study. Then how I can teach you?"
> But I was not to be put off so easily.
> Finally, he said, "Sometimes you can come and see me and I may have time to show you a few gestures." I came the next day and had a chat with the Manager, but I could not see Shankar.[50]

Although Louise was unable to get lessons from Shankar, her co-artist Madhavan gave her the address of a school in Kerala for training in Kathakali.

Louise told the *Woman's Weekly* that she intended to create a new Indian ballet on her return to Australia.[51] In order to bring more authenticity to her ballet, Louise got off the ship in Bombay (now Mumbai) to study Indian dance. Mary Louise Lightfoot observes that this was "strange for the time":

> Europe was heading for war. Women didn't travel much, especially on their own, and the "Dark Continent" of India, though a part of the British Empire was an unusual destination for a single white Australian woman.[52]

In her diary, she writes of her first introduction to Indian dance,

> My first introduction to traditional Indian dance was at the Fellowship School, showing "Manipuri" movements – lovely, graceful things of which I had seen nothing in Shankar's program, and very different from the virile Kathakali movements.[53]

Louise spent more than five months in India, where she again met Rukmini Devi Arundale in Adyar. Rukmini Devi was the first Indian Louise had met in Australia. Rukmini Devi's Kalakshetra Dance Academy, established in 1936, was one of the key players in the Bharatanatyam revival in India (Figure 3.8). On 16 March 1936, the *Hindu* reported Rukmini Devi's public debut recital of Bharatanatyam:

> A large and cultured audience assembled at Adyar yesterday to witness the exhibition of Bharata Natyam by Srimati Rukmini Devi. The occasion was notable as marking the public debut of an educated and cultural artiste from outside the ranks of the professional dancers.[54]

For the "educated and cultured" audiences, Rukmini Devi purified *Sadir* dance and replaced the sensual and carnal moves with innovation and religious emphasis. Louise light-heartedly describes her time with Rukmini in Adyar:

> After a couple of weeks, Rukmini came to watch my lesson. Knowing how amusing it can be to see an Oriental woman imitating a sylph. I could just imagine how comic I, a Westerner, looked when imitating a *devadasi*, so I quite forgave Rukmini's smiles. She was surprised that I could learn so much when I could not converse with the teacher.[55]

Soon, Misha and the students implored Louise to come back home. She reluctantly returned to Australia from India.

68  *The Australian mother of Kathakali*

*Figure 3.8* Rukmini Devi in a pose from Bharatanatyam
Photographer: Unknown
Source: *Rukmini Devi Arundale: Birth Centenary Volume* (2003)
Photograph Courtesy: Kalakshetra Foundation

After her return, Louise displayed the Indian costumes and dance movements to Misha and her students. She also started training her students to showcase on stage the story of the Indian God Krishna. In May 1938, Lightfoot-Burlakov produced their last joint recital – Louise's own "authentic Hindu style movement" version of *The Blue God* (about Indian gods and goddesses) with Indian costumes, ornaments and recorded *Vedic mantra* chantings sourced from India – at the NSW Conservatorium of Music (Figure 3.9).[56] Louise notes in her journal,

*Figure 3.9* (Top left to right) Gordon Hamilton and Colin McIntyre in First Australian Ballet's production of *The Blue God*, May 1938

Photograph: *PIX* Magazine

Source: Photograph from the Louise Lightfoot Bequest, Monash University

Photograph Courtesy: Music Archives of Monash University and Mary Louise Lightfoot

Only seven out of all our students mastered the Bharata Natya movements sufficiently to satisfy me, and these girls took the part of temple-devadasis, while about eighteen young girls danced Manipuri movements in inter-weaving circles, as offering bearers. Others joined in the crowd scenes. Our young men, eight of them, danced as religious fanatics, while a promising young student Gordon Hamilton danced the role of the *Blue God*.[57]

During the various shows of *The Blue God* in Sydney and Canberra, Louise was once again tempted to go back to India. She wrote,

> One day as I was idly turning the pages of a "Four Arts" magazine I had purchased the day of my first arrival in India, my eyes were suddenly focussed on a photograph printed therein – a photo of a school building. Underneath was written: "Keralakalamandalam, Cochin State, under the direction of the well-known Kerala Poet Vallathol."
> I wired my friend in India for details of the address of this famous man, and back came the information within a few days. I remembered how surprised I was that the long name of the school had been allowed in the wire as one word. I wrote to the school at once asking all about it, and whether I would be permitted to study there. A reply soon came from the secretary, Mukund Raja, and I was informed I would be most welcome at this interesting school.[58]

Mary Louise Lightfoot notes that Louise did not inform Misha about this development.[59] After *The Blue God*, Louise dissolved her partnership with Misha, packed her bags and returned to India – to the Malabar Coast (Kerala) – to find Kathakali.[60] Louise felt a bit relieved at this decision:

> After the show, I announced my intended departure, and our students were not very surprised.
> I booked a passage to India in the Stratheden leaving in October. Misha received the news surprisingly well. Of late he had begun to cherish ideas of reigning supreme in a school. I was never quite sure whether he meant it or not. Regarding my departure, I was unable to give him any idea of how long I would be absent, and I left it entirely to him to make his own arrangements during that time.[61]

Misha Burlakov continued the First Australian Ballet with the assistance of Barbara McDonnell, one of the company dancers and a teacher at the school.[62] During the 1940s, he produced *Lake of Swans*, a four-scene version of *Swan Lake*, which premiered at the Sydney Conservatorium. The First Australian Ballet disbanded in the 1950s, and Misha continued to teach at his own school until his death in 1965.[63]

Louise wrote a detailed account of her visit and life in Kerala. This was envisioned to be published later in a book of her adventures, entitled *Adventures in Kathakali*:

> Friends have sometimes wondered how I adapted myself so quickly to Indian village life. Perhaps adventure was already in my blood because my four grandparents were all adventurers to the "new" land of Australia. . . .
> For board and lodging, and whatever amount of tuition I liked to demand from the teachers, these kindly people charged me twenty-five rupees (two pounds and ten shillings in Australian money) per month![64]

Over the next half-decade, Louise lived in Kerala and Tamil Nadu, learning the different techniques of the sacred dance styles Kathakali and Bharatanatyam.[65] Louise, the first Australian and the first Western woman to study this art, immersed herself first in studying Kathakali, the traditional dance-drama performed at all-night performances in Hindu temples. She soon became a great publicist of Indian dance troupes and soloists by organising tours for troupes in South India and Ceylon (Sri Lanka) – Shivaram (1939, South India; 1943 and 1944, Ceylon); Asoka (1940, Bombay); Ramgopal (1940, Bangalore); Sreenivas Kulkarni's troupe (1943, Ceylon); and Neena Maya (1946, Calcutta). To support herself and the work, she taught classical ballet to children of the British Raj. She also worked with filmmaker K. Subramanyam at Madras (Chennai) and published widely her perspective pieces in the Indian press (Figure 3.10).

Alan Seymour noted that during her stay in India, the "religious tradition" and the "deep spiritual content of Indian dance" had

> an over-whelming effect upon her, and characteristically, she determined to learn everything she could about this profoundly exciting dance art . . . Lightfoot . . . absorbed its technique and emotional content until she was as conversant as possible with the background, traditions, and living spirit of Indian dancing.[66]

According to Moya Beaver, this was something that no Australian woman had done before.[67] Seymour also notes, not at all surprised, that Louise displayed that quintessential Australian trait of "initiative." He writes,

> unlike many Australians in the theatre world who have gone abroad and forgotten to come back, she has devotedly, and with passionate sincerity, attempted to bring something of culture, enlightenment, and international goodwill to the Australian people.[68]

Louise devoted her considerable talents – experiences drawn from promoting ballet in Australia – and energy to promoting Hindu or Indian classical dance (Figure 3.11). Seeing Louise's dedication towards promoting

*Figure 3.10* (Left to right) Louise Lightfoot and Ian C. Robson dancing on Europe Day at YWCA, Madras, India, 1938

Photographer: Unknown
Source: Photograph from the Louise Lightfoot Bequest, Monash University
Photograph Courtesy: Music Archives of Monash University and Mary Louise Lightfoot

*Figure 3.11* Louise Lightfoot wearing a sari
Photographer: Mac Juster
Source: Photograph from the Louise Lightfoot Bequest, Monash University
Photograph Courtesy: Music Archives of Monash University and Mary Louise Lightfoot

Kathakali, Vallathol Narayana Menon, the great poet of Malabar and the founder of Kerala Kalamandalam, bestowed upon Louise the fond title of "Kathakali's Australian mother."[69]

Louise was thrilled by the whole experience of learning Kathakali – involving poetry, song, acting and dance – and soon she appealed to both the British in India to appreciate Indian dance and to Indian parents to allow their sons and daughters to dance. While she learnt dancing and organised tours for Indian artists at Kalamandalam, Louise was also busy publishing in Indian, British and Australian newspapers and magazines regarding Hindu dance art, her journey to Kalamandalam, the Indian way of life and other relevant socio-cultural issues.[70]

In 1940, she published an "International Appeal of the Ballet" in the *Hindu* (February 11):

> We can help in the cause of art by making a fuss of these artists and their splendid work, which will soon make Indian Ballet a powerful influence on the whole world of Ballet. We are preparing the world – so we hope – for an international understanding, and there is nothing more completely international in its appeal than Ballet.[71]

In 1946, Louise published a piece on Kathakali in an Australian newspaper, the *Argus* (July 31, 1946), titled "Two Thousand Years of Rhythm." She writes,

> Educated young women, including the daughter of the first woman member the Legislative Assembly, are studying Kathakali. Even though they haven't much knowledge of it yet, they are enthralling the sophisticated, cinema-loving audiences of India's big cities.[72]

One of the reasons for Louise's remark and explanation of the limited interest of Indians, and of only a handful of Western dancers, in Kathakali is the time and dedication needed to be a trained Kathakali artist. She noted of her own time spent studying this art in Kerala,

> Training for Kathakali is a trial of strength . . . No European dancer would care to rise at 4 every morning to practise two hours of eye movements near a little lamp in the darkness. Or to sit for another two hours clapping out intricate rhythms based on bars of five and seven, and other difficult beats. Or to deliberately submit to the painful oil massages necessary to limber the body. They groan and weep over those massages, and they have to memorise the stanzas of the vocal accompaniment to over a hundred all night ballets. That goes on for eight years, then the real dancing begins.[73]

Louise also realised at a very early stage that Kathakali would never be "adopted entirely by Western dancers" and audiences, because it "wouldn't suit them."[74] It was a subject quite new for Australians despite the fact that

> we are so close to India here, we know comparatively nothing of the art of this great ancient land. It is not our fault exactly. We are not educated to think that there is anything of particular interest for us in this neighbouring country.[75]

Therefore, it was best to infuse the Indian rhythms of this symbolic art with Western dance and vice versa. Here, Louise's knowledge and training in architecture, sculpture and painting helped her in the elaborate planning of costumes, ornaments and stage design. Nevertheless, this experimentation would not have been possible without the active support of Ananda Shivaram – Louise's teacher, friend and star artist.

## Notes

1. Parts of this chapter have appeared as "Introduction" in *Louise Lightfoot in Search of India: An Australian Dancer's Experience*, compiled and edited by Amit Sarwal (2017). Published here with the permission of Cambridge Scholars Publishing.
2. To compile Louise's biography, I have used material from Lightfoot and Quartly, "Lightfoot, Louisa Mary (1902–1979)," 2005; Lightfoot, "Lightfoot, Louise," 2008; NLAdance, "Indian Dance in Australia," 2010; Brissenden and Glennon, *Australia Dances*, 2010; Lightfoot, *Lightfoot Dancing*, 2015.
3. Lightfoot, *Lightfoot Dancing*, Chapter 5.
4. Founded in 1902 in East Melbourne by the Sisters of Charity, Catholic Ladies' College shifted to Eltham in 1971.
5. See Lightfoot and Quartly, "Lightfoot, Louisa Mary (1902–1979)," 2005.
6. Walter Burley Griffin was an American architect and landscape architect, who is best known for his role in designing Canberra, Australia's capital city. Griffin visited Lucknow (India) in the 1930s and was inspired by the architecture and culture of India. He died of peritonitis in early 1937, five days after gall bladder surgery at King George's Hospital in Lucknow, and was buried in Christian Cemetery in Lucknow.
7. Lightfoot, *Lightfoot Dancing*, Chapter 6.
8. Castlecrag was originally planned by Walter Burley Griffin, who named the suburb after a towering crag of rock overlooking Middle Harbour, known locally as Edinburgh Castle. Griffin came to Castlecrag in 1925 after tiring of the politics surrounding the implementation of his designs for Australia's capital city, Canberra.
9. Lightfoot, *Lightfoot Dancing*, Chapter 7.
10. See Lightfoot and Quartly, "Lightfoot, Louisa Mary (1902–1979)," 2005.
11. Ibid.
12. Lightfoot, *Lightfoot Dancing*, Chapter 6.
13. Ibid.
14. Ibid.
15. See Lightfoot and Quartly, "Lightfoot, Louisa Mary (1902–1979)," 2005.
16. Lightfoot, *Lightfoot Dancing*, Chapter 7.
17. Pavlova's company presented nineteen ballet pieces including *Don Quixote*, *The Magic Flute* and *Autumn Leaves*. See Ibid.
18. Misha (or Mischa) Burlakov was born in Ukraine and came to Australia in 1913. He had performed national and folk dances for various clubs and schools and also appeared in classical ballet recitals in NSW. See Brissenden and Glennon, *Australia Dances*, 82.
19. See Lightfoot and Quartly, "Lightfoot, Louisa Mary (1902–1979)," 2005.
20. See Lightfoot, "Lightfoot, Louise," 2008.
21. Lightfoot, *Lightfoot Dancing*, Chapter 7.

22 Ibid., Chapter 8.
23 "The First Australian Ballet (1929–1950)," 2010.
24 See Brissenden and Glennon, *Australia Dances*, 82–83.
25 The *Indian* Section of the *Theosophical* Society's international headquarters is at Adyar in Chennai, India, and has been in existence in Australia since 1895. For a detailed discussion, see Roe, *Beyond Belief*, 1986.
26 See Lightfoot, "Lightfoot, Louise," 2008.
27 See Brissenden and Glennon, *Australia Dances*, 82; Lightfoot and Quartly, "Lightfoot, Louisa Mary (1902–1979)," 2005.
28 Lightfoot, *Lightfoot Dancing*, 2015.
29 Ibid., Chapter 9.
30 *Coppélia* is a comic ballet originally choreographed by Arthur Saint-Léon to the music of Léo Delibes, with libretto by Charles Nuitter. Nuitter's libretto and mise-en-scène were based upon two stories by E. T. A. Hoffmann: *Der Sandmann* (The Sandman), and *Die Puppe* (The Doll). *Coppélia* concerns an inventor, Dr Coppelius, who has made a life-size dancing doll. It is so lifelike that Franz, a village swain, becomes infatuated with it and sets aside his true heart's desire, Swanhilde. She shows him his folly by dressing as the doll, pretending to make it come to life and ultimately saving him from an untimely end at the hands of the inventor.
31 See Brissenden and Glennon, *Australia Dances*, 82.
32 Lightfoot, *Lightfoot Dancing*, Chapter 9.
33 Lawson, "The First Australian Ballet," 1998; See also Lightfoot, "Lightfoot, Louise," 2008.
34 Lightfoot, *Lightfoot Dancing*, Chapter 9.
35 The cost of attending a dance class at their studio was around one to two shillings. See Ibid.
36 *Petrushka* (*Pétrouchka*) is a ballet set to music by the Russian composer Igor Stravinsky. It was composed in 1910–1911 and revised in 1947. The ballet tells the story of a Russian traditional puppet Petrushka, who is made of straw, with a bag of sawdust as his body, but who comes to life and develops emotions.
37 See Brissenden and Glennon, *Australia Dances*, 83.
38 Beaver cited in Lightfoot, *Lightfoot Dancing*, Chapter 9.
39 See Brissenden and Glennon, *Australia Dances*, 83.
40 Lightfoot, *Lightfoot Dancing*, Chapter 9.
41 Ibid., Chapter 10.
42 See Lightfoot, "Lightfoot, Louise," 2008.
43 Ibid.
44 Quoted in Gibson, "Dancer's Dream Lives On," 1999.
45 See Lightfoot, "Lightfoot, Louise," 2008.
46 Lightfoot, *Lightfoot Dancing*, Chapter 2.
47 Ibid.
48 Ibid.
49 Ibid.
50 Ibid.
51 See Lightfoot and Quartly, "Lightfoot, Louisa Mary (1902–1979)," 2005.
52 Lightfoot, *Lightfoot Dancing*, Chapter 1.
53 Ibid., Chapter 11.
54 Quoted in Katrak, *Contemporary Indian Dance*, 30.
55 Lightfoot, *Lightfoot Dancing*, Chapter 11.

56 Louise used Manipuri dance steps learned from Rajkumar Priyagopal Singh's father, Maharaja Surjaboro Singh, to create the choreography of *The Blue God*.
57 Lightfoot, *Lightfoot Dancing*, Chapter 11.
58 Ibid.
59 Ibid.
60 Involving the unfolding of stories in dance or dance-drama, Kathakali originated from *Krishnanattam* (Sanskrit plays in praise of Lord Krishna) and *Ramanattam* or Attakatha (Malayalam plays in praise of Lord Rama) in the coastal state of Kerala during the seventeenth century. Kathakali does not include any onstage dialogue at all and is noted chiefly for being an all-male domain (even female roles are played by men). The variety and range of characters – from noble heroes to demons – and religious themes and stories concerning the victory of good over evil are drawn from *Mahabharata*, the *Ramayana*, and the *Puranas*.
61 Lightfoot, *Lightfoot Dancing*, Chapter 11.
62 Brissenden and Glennon, *Australia Dances*, 84.
63 Ibid.
64 Lightfoot, *Lightfoot Dancing*, Chapter 12.
65 See Lightfoot and Quartly, "Lightfoot, Louisa Mary (1902–1979)," 2005.
66 Seymour, "Presenting Louise Lightfoot," 51.
67 Moya Beaver also taught at this Sydney-based school and in the 1930s, in absence of Lightfoot and Burlakov, when they went to Europe, ran it as the acting principal. See Beaver, "Interview with Michelle Potter," 1994.
68 Seymour, "Presenting Louise Lightfoot," 51.
69 "Australian *Kathakali* Artiste Dead," 1979.
70 Lightfoot, *Lightfoot Dancing*, Chapter 15.
71 Lightfoot, "International Appeal of the Ballet," 1940.
72 Lightfoot, "Two Thousand Years of Rhythm," 16.
73 Ibid.
74 Ibid.
75 See Lightfoot, "Explanation of Items by Miss Lightfoot's Hindu Dance Group," 1947b.

# 4   The dancing God[1]

In 1938, Louise Lightfoot arrived at the Kerala Kalamanadalam and recorded her first observation thus:

> I hope anyone visiting the land of Kathakali will arrive at his destination in the dawn, as I did. Apart from the particular loveliness of dawn in that country, it was the dawn of a new kind of life that will never be forgotten. Maybe the arduous journey I had experienced made my arrival all the sweeter. Certainly, it was the happiest dawn I had ever known, and it was filled with a sense of "coming home."[2]

Here, she adapted quickly to the Kerala village life and ascribed it to the adventurous spirit of her grandparents. She wrote,

> Friends have sometimes wondered how I adapted myself so quickly to Indian village life. Perhaps adventure was already in my blood because my four grandparents were all adventurers in the "new" land of Australia.[3]

Louise's teacher Kunju Nair did not speak English and used Sanskrit words to teach Kathakali. A fellow student named Krishnamurty, who knew a bit of English, was appointed as an interpreter for Louise. Every day, she would wake up at 6 am to get ready for her 8 am training in "a cool, palm-thatched shed."[4] Here, she also made a point to watch as many Kathakali performances as possible by accompanying the Kalamandalam troupe. But soon she needed money to survive in Kerala and therefore started looking for some work to sustain herself:

> Having savoured a taste of Kathakali, I decided to follow its call and settle in India near Kerala. I ascertained that the nearest hill-station that had European colleges was at Ootacamund in the Nilgiri ranges above Kerala. There I would try to earn a living by teaching, so that I could continue my studies under a Kathakali master.[5]

*The dancing God* 79

Apart from studying Kathakali, Krishnamurty encouraged Louise to use her skills in troupe management to establish her own troupe of Kathakali dancers.

In 1939, Krishnamurty introduced Louise to a very talented young dancer at Kalamanadalam. This extraordinary dancer was Ananda Shivaram, who studied as well as tutored Kathakali dance at this institution. Louise noted that as a substitute teacher for Kunju Nair and Madhavan, Shivaram was hopeless and an utter disappointment (Figure 4.1).[6] But when she saw Shivaram essaying the role of Krishna in a dance-drama based on the Indian epic *Mahabharata*, her feelings were out of this world. She was so captivated by Shivaram that she wanted to keep him forever.

*Figure 4.1* Ananda Shivaram, 1947

Photographer: Unknown

Source: Photograph from the Louise Lightfoot Bequest, Monash University

Photograph Courtesy: Music Archives of Monash University and Mary Louise Lightfoot

Soon after seeing Shivaram in Kathakali, I felt a wish to stretch out my hand and capture that little creature. Then I would always have Kathakali in the palm of my hand. I could turn on happiness any time, I thought – as if we could capture what is in a bird![7]

Shivaram, born in 1916 in the upper-caste Nayar or Nair community of Kerala, commenced his *gurukulam* (residential school) training at the age of eight under the guidance of his father, Gopala Panicker (Pannikar), a learned master of dancing and acting (Figure 4.2).[8]

*Figure 4.2* Ananda Shivaram with his father and first guru, Gopala Panikar
Photographer: Unknown
Source: Photograph from the Louise Lightfoot Bequest, Monash University
Photograph Courtesy: Music Archives of Monash University and Mary Louise Lightfoot

Charming and lively, he [Gopala Panicker] had been a Kathakali actor all his life. He had learnt in his own village from a wealthy cultured land-owner who taught a few boys in his home, a few doors away from the family's present ancestral home . . . Shivaram learnt first at the age of eight from his father in his own compound.⁹

In 1929, impressed by Shivaram's performance at the Chittur Sreekrishna Temple, Poet Vallathol Menon and Mukund Raja offered him free training in Kathakali at Kerala Kalamandalam (Figure 4.3). As a young man,

*Figure 4.3* Poet Vallathol Narayana Menon
Source: Kerala Kalamandalam
Photograph Courtesy: Vallathol Museum and Kerala Kalamandalam

Shivaram performed in India and Ceylon with Indian dance troupes, but he desired to go abroad and establish himself as an exponent of Kathakali in Europe. He tried very hard to arrange for a solo tour of Western countries, but the intervention of the Second World War ruined his plans.[10]

In a world replete with distrust, emptiness and mindless destruction, Louise was mesmerised by Shivaram's excellence in dance, personality and spiritual attachment to his art. She wrote,

> I came to realise that Shivaram was the perfect medium to receive the spirit of Kathakali from above and give it out to us undistorted by anything in his character. As a friend in Australia put it, "He gives a feeling of crystalline purity coming down from above."[11]

Louise thought of him as the very epitome and "embodiment of the Indian spirit of dancing."[12] She noted that for Shivaram, a true Hindu dancer, and others like him,

> dancing means more than entertainment. It is considered an approach to God. That does not mean it is a very serious and boring affair. It means that the Hindu understands the real meaning of beauty and the true function of art in life. The Hindu temple was the home of the arts of music, sculpture, painting and dancing, as well as philosophy.[13]

It was at this point that Louise thought of bringing him to Australia.[14] Louise's initial feeling was that to comprehend the Indian art and artists' triumph over destruction, her own country must see Shivaram and enjoy Kathakali dance dramas as a cathartic experience. In an interview with Alan Seymour, she explained her reasons for bringing Shivaram to Australia:

> The World in its present tortured state desperately needs people of goodwill, people who offer enlightenment and a creative way as an answer to the contemporary mania for destruction and violence. ... [A]rt and artists can forge strong links between the peoples of all countries, assisting to promote understanding and mutual goodwill, in place of the national distrust which nowadays so largely prevails.[15]

Louise believed that dancing, for Shivaram, meant far more than entertainment. Realising that their audiences were uninitiated, they sought to make Shivaram's performances of Kathakali popular and to distil the whole experience of watching Indian dance-drama into a cathartic one. Their goal was to communicate the ideas of Hindu spirituality embedded in Kathakali while removing some of the complex religious context associated with it.[16]

Shivaram was not pleased with the way Kathakali was then being used for onstage performances, lacking in full costume and makeup. Louise writes,

> It seemed to him impudent that he should imagine the audience interested in himself, rather than in a great character of Kathakali. I could not quite understand this then, but I came to understand that Kathakali tries to eliminate the individual and concentrate on the universal, while our theatrical art brings forward the individual who, under the circumstances, needs to be saturated with self-confidence.[17]

It is clear why Louise and Shivaram collaborated. In going to India for training and then returning as an accomplished impresario, Lightfoot demonstrated the quintessential Australian trait of "initiative." According to Seymour,

> moreover, unlike many Australians in the theatre world who [had] gone abroad [particularly to the U.K., U.S.A. and Europe] and forgotten to come back, she ... devotedly, and with passionate sincerity, attempted to bring something of culture, enlightenment, and international goodwill to the Australian people.[18]

For his part, Shivaram, who was trying to reach out to a wider audience and to establish a niche for himself in the dance world, cynically described his reasons for looking toward the West to an Australian journalist:

> Indian dancing used to be a most lucrative profession but since the advent of Scotch whiskey dancing is becoming less popular with the wealthy Indians, and more and more Indian dancers are looking to the Western world for occupation.[19]

As evident, the reasons for the decline in the patronage of Kathakali had to do with the political economy of colonial relations, extending far beyond the "advent of Scotch whiskey."[20] Shivaram's allusion to "Scotch whiskey" can be read as a symbol of exploitative colonial relations that led to the popularity of Western dance forms or Western-influenced (corrupted) *nautch* dance among Indians.

Dance historian and theorist Uttara Asha Coorlawala has argued that such an open appeal on the part of Indian artists represents a hunger for "international exposure" and a desire to achieve "dignity" or a sense of cultural identity for India – "a battered nation emerging from centuries of economic and cultural exploitation."[21] International acclaim has often improved the reception of many Indian dancers in India. Coorlawala asserts that, even today, dancers who are celebrated abroad and gain international exposure often "return to a new level of acceptance and respect for their art within India," as their dance, which has been approved by critics and audiences abroad, is now "perceived as epitomizing the highest values of Indian culture."[22]

Lightfoot persuaded Shivaram to experiment, to create shorter versions of dance-dramas, and to adapt ancient Kathakali works to modern tastes with her Hindu Dance Group in Australia. In fact, the experimentation started in the late-1930s, when Louise and Shivaram, with the help of Stella Kramrisch, a well-known American curator and interpreter of Indian art and the key figure behind the Indian Society of Oriental Art, performed at Ramakrishna Mission. Louise produced a shorter version of Kathakali to audiences' amazement.

> We trimmed the Kathakali performance down to two and a half-hours for the English and Bengali audiences – just the highlights. Stella Kramrisch (the moving spirit of the Indian Society of Oriental Art) and I were careful to see that lamp oil was not kept on stage in a kerosene tin, that followers did not stand near the stage or walk across, that bell and costume strings were neatly tied. Fortunately, no attempt was made to alter the traditional lighting, setting or costumes.[23]

Mary Louise Lightfoot notes that these "presentations used a similar format to Louise's Australian productions."[24] Lightfoot and Shivaram, rather than having all-night performances of major Hindu epics, then went for the new Westernised form, which mixed short scenes from different epics. The other strategy used was the inclusion of different folk and classical dances. Such a suggestion from Lightfoot seems surprising, considering the highly codified performance associated with Kathakali. But this experimentation would have been considered appropriate by Kathakali lovers and critics.[25]

In 1939, famous Indian dancer and choreographer Ram Gopal (a.k.a. Bissano Ram Gopal), along with his partner, an Indonesian dancer, Retna Mohini, visited Kalamandalam to meet Poet Vallathol. Ram Gopal has performed mostly as a soloist and blended the Indian classical dance with balletic choreography (Figure 4.4).[26] Along with Uday Shankar, he was among the first to showcase Hindu temple dance in the West, starting in the 1930s.[27] He was invited to the United States by La Meri to tour with her through Asia in the 1930s. In her obituary of Ram Gopal, Leela Venkatraman wrote,

> Pictures of Ram Gopal turned out in the briefest of skin-tight shorts, with necklaces adorning his magnificent torso and an exotic headgear crowning the dignified head have become one of the indelible dance images. Ram Gopal's dance transcended gender and regional

*Figure 4.4* Portrait of Indian dancer Ram Gopal, April 21, 1938

Photographer: Carl Van Vechten

Source: www.loc.gov/pictures/item/2004662942/. Collection: Carl Van Vechten Photographs

Photograph Courtesy: Library of Congress Prints and Photographs Division Washington, D.C.

boundaries. Turned out in exotic costumes, in all probability designed by Western garment experts, Ram Gopal's dance represented not so much a form like Bharatanatyam, Kathak or Kathakali, as an essential Indianness he was trying to convey to western audiences. Strangely, even with his love for the classical vocabulary, he chose to make his home in the West and not in India – which he visited regularly. Perhaps the different Western context gave his creative imagination freedom without tying him down to the orthodox presentation conventions associated with each traditional form.[28]

Ram Gopal showed a keen interest in taking Shivaram as part of his troupe to perform abroad. An excited Shivaram broke this news to Louise, who was saddened by it, as his departure would jeopardise her own plans. Louise wrote,

> There was nothing to be done. I could only congratulate Shivaram and weep for myself. My bird, my treasure, was to be shipped overseas. Shivaram was to leave India a few weeks after Ram Gopal's departure for Paris and London. Knowing I was upset, Ram assured me that Shivaram would return to the school in six months' time.[29]

But as fate would have it, Poet Vallathol agreed to send Shivaram on one condition, that Ram Gopal should submit a donation of Rupees 2000 to Kerala Kalmandalam, which was going through a monetary crisis. The donation never arrived. Louise observed that "the newspapers rang with the success of Ram abroad, but the carefree life of Kalamandalam went on as usual and Shivaram remained."[30] But all was not well in this little carefree world of Kalamandalam. Louise was not paid her dues, and Poet Vallathol stopped the institution's performers and musicians from working with her. However, Shivaram was unable to balance both teaching and performing roles. These circumstances led to the departure of Louise and Shivaram from the institution and the beginning of their venture on the Indian stage. Louise wrote about the misfortunes: "For the first time in India, I now wished I were safely home in Melbourne, never to roam again."[31] However, in spite of it, Louise did not leave India.

Louise and Shivaram moved to Madras from where she continued writing in newspapers on various topics, teaching ballet and organising local tours for Shivaram as a publicist (Figure 4.5).

> Our first Kathakali lecture-demonstration at Madras University brought Shivaram into the public eye . . . His first solo recital at a private home was followed by an invitation from the well-known music society the R. R. Sabha. For that performance, Shivaram searched in vain for a girl

The dancing God 87

*Figure 4.5* An advertisement for a dance recital by Ananda Shivaram and Louise Lightfoot at the All India Khadi and Swadeshi Exhibition, Trichinopoly, India, 1939

Photograph Courtesy: Music Archives of Monash University and Mary Louise Lightfoot

to assist him as a partner. The situation for respectable girls appearing on the stage was very much like it had been in our early Victorian days.

We decided that my pupils and I would have to come to the rescue and supply ballet items between Shivaram's items.[32]

Despite critical acclaim coming their way, both Louise and Shivaram found that earning money was emerging as a bigger problem. Louise got in touch with Uday Shankar's brother, Rajendra, with a request to accept Shivaram as a resident performer at Shankar's newly opened India Culture Centre in Almora, North India.[33] After visiting the centre, Louise thought of taking admission as a private student for beginner's classes in Bharatanatyam but was refused by the secretary of the institute: "No European students are being admitted to the Centre for five years. You may apply for special permission if you wish and your application will go before the committee."[34] After a few days, Louise was invited to appear before an interview board consisting of an American administrator and Uday Shankar. Louise explained her case and the reason behind her interest in taking admission at the centre. Shankar asked Louise, "You might perhaps teach Indian dancing there [in Australia] when you go back, and produce Indian ballet?"[35] Louise responded positively, and Shankar decided that Louise could not take admission at the centre, keeping in mind the "dreadful things Le Meri had done in New York."[36] While Shivaram stayed inside the centre, Louise managed to get accommodation outside and continued her writing and making plans for Shivaram. As Shivaram got busy in his new roles and learning, Louise got a letter from Asoka (a.k.a. Ernst Rubener), a German dancer based in India.[37] Inspired by the work and fame of Uday Shankar, Asoka had travelled to India in the 1930s to learn Bharatanatyam. He invited Louise to join him and organise a tour for him and his partner. Shivaram could not believe that Louise had decided to leave him alone in Almora and move to Bombay.

While Louise was in Bombay, she saw the effects of World War II in India. Foreigners, especially Germans, were rounded up and sent to camps for aliens, organised by the British Indian Army. Asoka, along with his German friends, was taken away, and Louise was out of work. She couldn't forget the sight of people being taken away. Despite all the challenging situations and events, she was still not ready to leave India. She writes,

> I shall never forget the expression on the face of one woman as she saw her husband being taken away with Asoka. A taste of war! I was at the right port if I wanted to sail now, but somehow I knew I wasn't going to.[38]

Louise then moved to a hostel run by nuns. To earn a living in Bombay, she started giving radio talks on *Do You Know, Madame?*, a program broadcast at 1:35 pm and writing on art for the *Bombay Chronicle* for very small fees.[39]

By the end of August 1940, Louise was fed up with her gigs at the radio and newspaper. She wanted to be back in action with Kathakali. While lying on complete bedrest because of a high fever, she received a surprise visit from dancer Ram Gopal. With the support of wealthy patrons, Ram Gopal had been to Japan, the United States, France and Britain.[40] But the war had put a stop to his foreign tours, and he was in Bombay to scout for talent to form a new dance troupe in Bangalore. He offered Louise a role as assistant organiser, free tuition in Indian dance and Rupees 50 a month as pocket money. Louise accepted Ram Gopal's offer and was happy to go back to pursuing her passion. However, in her excitement and happiness, she didn't forget Shivaram:

> By evening Ram Gopal arrived with a taxi and soon I was lying comfortably in a first-class compartment, sipping very hot cocoa and

regaling the amused Ram with the story of Sister's appearance at my door. Then it was his turn to talk, and how he could talk! He described how he danced and danced as one possessed. I lay back satisfied that I had found my real work at last. Perhaps Shivaram would help us one day with his Kathakali.[41]

The next few years were full of adventure with Ram Gopal and his troupe. Louise wrote to J. C. Williamson's theatrical firm regarding bringing Ram Gopal's Indian dance troupe to Australia. But the firm thought that at that point in time, bringing an authentic Indian dance and music troupe "might not be appreciated."[42]

Soon, adventures with Ram Gopal came to end with a bitter fight. The issue was that Louise, who was also once again trying to branch out as a ballet teacher in India, in one of her lectures at a leading European Girls' School, did not disclose her relation with Ram Gopal's Indian dance school. Ram Gopal became angry on noticing the newspaper reports about Louise's talk without a mention of his name or school. Louise apologised to Ram Gopal, left his school and moved into a guesthouse run by a Quaker woman in the Bangalore Cantonment area. After this bitter experience with Ram Gopal, Shivaram was once again in Louise's thoughts:

> I dumped my trunks gratefully and opened up a large tube-like parcel I had just received from in the post. It contained an oil painting of Shivaram by an American living not far from the Shankar Cultural Centre in Almora. I nailed the canvas up on the wall. The pose was stiff, the head turned sideways. It would have been fine if the head had suddenly turned and smiled.[43]

In Bangalore, Louise once again started actively teaching ballet to English and Anglo-Indian children of the British Raj at the residence of an English colonel.[44]

Shivaram, who was no longer working with Uday Shankar, as he was not getting solo performances as promised, sent a letter to Louise stating that he had resigned from the centre. He planned to meet Louise in Bangalore and then head off to his home in Kerala. Louise was glad to hear from Shivaram, but when she saw him, her heart sank:

> A *jatka* (two-wheeled horse carriage) rattled into the guest-house compound the day he was due to arrive. My heart bumped with delight and horror when a skinny, dark-skinned Indian jumped down. He was dirty from three days third class train travel, wearing a pair of check European pants, a khaki flannel shirt hanging out over them, his long

hair slicked back behind his ears, and his face grinning timid before the white Memsahib. Was this the great dancer, Shivaram?[45]

Louise was happy to know that Shivram was ready to forget the style taught by Uday Shankar and go back to a pure Kathakali routine. They both left the guesthouse and moved into a rented flat for ten shillings a week only to realise in the night that it was part of a dairy with cows mooing and creating a racket.[46] After some time, Shivaram left for Kerala, and Louise continued teaching ballet to her pupils.

In 1941, Shivaram returned to Bangalore along with his drummer, Variar. He started giving Louise lessons in Kathakali. They also organised a few Kathakali and Kummi folk dance programs for stage. One of their programs was in aid of the war fund, under the royal patronage of His Highness the Maharaja of Mysore and the British resident in Mysore.

> Though both Shivaram and I were tired by rehearsals, teaching, cycling in the heat to the City, distributing posters and tickets, erecting a proscenium and doing a hundred other things, it proved a great success. Divided strictly into two parts, half was ballet provided by my dear little pupils in white tutus and half was Indian dancing by Shivaram and myself.[47]

After a few more charity performances, both saved enough to go on a Christmas holiday to Kerala. In Shivaram's village, Louise met his parents and saw a local troupe perform traditional Kathakali dance-dramas.

While the war was raging and Indian nationalism was at its peak, Louise, now back in Bangalore as a full-time teacher at Bishop Cotton's Girls' School, was busy writing for newspapers and planning ways to promote Kathakali abroad. However, Shivaram did not support her idea of going abroad. A frustrated Louise observed that even with growing competition amongst dancers in Bangalore and nearby towns, Shivaram was happy with what he had. She writes,

> In my spare time, I began to work on the idea of lecture-demonstrations abroad for I felt sure that the war must end soon. [It didn't.] But I got little cooperation from Shivaram about this – his main interest seemed to be in helping poor people from his own caste to get jobs in Bangalore . . .
>
> Shivaram could spend hours talking and joking with his pals. He had a love of ease and showed no desire to read and improve his mind. Unlike other up and coming dancers in the vicinity, he made no attempt at forming business contacts for prospective shows or tuition. One

was loath to scold him as he had such a charming nature, such that his absence made us sad and everyone looked forward to his return.[48]

To Louise, Shivaram now represented a flower which was living and growing in an uncongenial environment:

> He was like a delicate flower, to be cherished and admired, and usually quite timid and unassertive. Now this flower began to wilt in an unsuitable atmosphere and as the year went on he became thin and quiet.[49]

Shivaram tried forming a dance troupe with Kulkarni, his former pupil and a choreographer for films in Madras. But after only a few months, Shivaram's health deteriorated, and she brought him back to Bangalore. At this point, Louise realised that to fulfill their ambition and dream of performing authentic Hindu dance abroad, they didn't need a full troupe. Louise decided,

> I realised that Shivaram had not the mental or physical strength for continuous teaching and producing. Like many ballet dancers I knew, he must wait till the organsiers, the musicians, choreographer, producer, lighting expert, stage manager, artistic director, publicity manager and the dresser had all done their work. Then he would come and dance in the breeze like a flower and give a vision of unearthly beauty to all.
> If he would shine, I felt I must be the man, or men, behind the scenes and do the work. For I alone realised the preciousness of the instrument in my care, and how exquisitely the ideals of ancient India could be played through him. How then could I find some opportunity for Shivaram to shine through my presentations?[50]

In 1943, Louise and Shivaram's first tour abroad to Ceylon (Sri Lanka) with Kulkarni's troupe materialised, but it was a misadventure from the very beginning – their papers were misplaced by local police, resulting in a delay at port, a contractor cancelled their opening shows, an agent ran away with box office collection and there was a case against a contractor for payment. But they took all this in good spirits, once the newspapers praised Shivaram's performance. A Colombo-based dance critic wrote,

> The focal point of the evening was the performance of Shivaram. With perfect rhythm of body, rapid use of feet and fingers – with a meaning in each of their movements – Shivaram dances with grace, skill and fire added by a romantic handsomeness, a lithe body and that radiance which is the hallmark of personality.[51]

However, as a spoilsport, the local contractor filed a counter-case of cheating on Kulkarni. So, despite good reviews and some other local performances, the troupe decided to secretly escape from Ceylon to India, to avoid further court summons and harassment at the hands of a rogue contractor. After a few more shows in South India's small towns, Louise went back to teaching and Shivaram joined a well-known film producer, K. Subramaniam, as choreographer along with training two girls in Madras to expand his troupe.[52]

In 1944, they assembled a small troupe with a couple of experts in Kalaripayat (or Kalaripayattu - a traditional martial arts from Kerala), three girls, three musicians (two drummers and one flautist), two of whom worked in an aircraft factory as workers, and some others, including background dancers, singers, their guardians and managers. In all, a troupe of sixteen people proceeded to Ceylon, only to be told by the Protector of Emigrants' office that Louise's passport needed a stamp from the Madras Home Department. After almost a week of waiting, Louise marched back to Madras to meet the resident. She got her passport endorsed and made it back to Jaffna to meet other members of the troupe. Like her first epic tour of Ceylon, this one also met the same fate. Disease, jealousy, rumours, back-stabbing and fraud claims by the local contractor made touring in Ceylon tough for Louise and Shivaram.

> My flautist fell in love with the Kathakali actor's sister and passed her a ring one night. The brother discovered it and beat her. The Kathakali actor himself had become jealous of Shivaram's position as solo dancer and demanded, and was given a solo. The Contractor's face was often flushed with drinking and he joined forces with the troupe members showing an aversion for me. He spread rumours that my demand for a big sum of money (mostly to be pocketed by my wicked self) was ruining his chances of touring, and that I prevented him from booking shows. He finally announced he did not intend paying me, but was going to claim damages from me.[53]

Louise sought the advice of an Indian agent in Ceylon, who agreed to mediate between the fighting parties. He got Louise's money back and also divided them into two troupes – one to follow Louise and the other to go with the local contractor. After this episode, Louise pledged "never again" to tour with an Indian dance troupe.[54]

Louise and Shivaram returned to Madras and met with filmmaker K. Subramaniam with an eye to bagging a role for Shivaram and his new female dance partner. Shivaram got a role in the film along with Kamini Kumar Sinha, a Bharatnatyam and Manipuri dancer and Louise's first teacher in Madras, and Gopinath, a talented senior from Kerala Kalamanadalam.

Shivaram requested the filmmaker to sign Louise as well in some capacity. Subramaniam offered a generous salary and engaged Louise as his director of art and publicity at the Madras United Artist Corporation (MUAC). The film was *Narthana Murali*. Keeping in mind the theme and story of the film, Louise was hopeful that Shivaram would get the leading role as Lord Krishna and it would be an advantage for her to introduce him to Australia – as an Indian dancer and film star. But modest Shivaram was delegated to the background, behind the flamboyant and domineering dancer Gopinath's men. Louise was angry but continued with her job with Subramaniam, with one goal in mind – to save enough to take Shivaram abroad.

> K. Subramaniam knew well my opinion that Shivaram was the ideal Lord Krishna, but the very idea was unthinkable! It was traditional in Madras district to dress up a pretty young woman as the God Krishna, loading her with ornaments and garlands and adoring her to their hearts' content [while in Kathakali, female parts were still taken by men]. Hence a student of Gopinath's got the divine role of Krishna as the flute-player. After this crime I quite lost faith in the artistic integrity of my boss; but because our salaries went on and world peace had been declared and I need money to take Shivaram to Australia, we therefore continued our jobs at MUAC.[55]

The production problems led to this film being shelved, and soon, most of the people involved in filming and artists resigned, including Louise. However, Shivaram and his partner remained with the film company.

In September 1945, as soon as World War II ended, Louise sailed for Australia, intent on bringing Hindu dance to her country. She was a bit anxious about the reception of an authentic Hindu dancer in White Australia. Louise wrote,

> How would Australian people appreciate this living temple fresco I was bringing to them? Would they be interested in a Museum of Temple Art tucked into a little dark man? Would they realise the importance of it all, and link it with plans for future world-peace?
>
> Much depended on me as Impresario and would-be missionary of Hindu Culture. I began negotiations for a permit to bring my treasure to White Australia. I knew better than to ask financial help from either India or Australia – that might delay me many years and end in disappointment. Shivaram must come alone.[56]

When Louise's mother heard that she was bringing a Hindu dancer to Australia, she sent a message: "On no account bring a coloured gentleman with you! You would be very much misunderstood."⁵⁷ Similar feelings were expressed by the British resident in Madras. Shivaram told Mary Louise Lightfoot that on seeing the big English resident, he tried to hide behind Louise. The resident was not at all encouraging and told Louise in a cold manner, "Only cricketers from India go to Australia. I've never heard of any artist from India going there."⁵⁸ But Louise was adamant and Shivaram loyal to the cause. Louise soon contacted the Indian high commissioner in Australia, Sir Raghunath Paranjpye, and through his request, Shivaram got permission to stay in Australia on a six-month visa. But their troubles were not yet over. It took years to complete the necessary paperwork – birth certificates, police verification and passport – for Shivaram. Louise wrote,

> Likewise, the P&O shipping agents in Bombay [now Mumbai] and Calcutta [now Kolkata] had no hopes of getting us passages to Australia because there were eight hundred names ahead of ours on the list. They thought it might be a year before we got away! Fares were still at First Class rates only.⁵⁹

During the waiting period, Louise travelled to Calcutta to join Shivaram and also study Bharatanatyam from Ellappa – a renowned teacher from Madras, who had trained many *devadasis*. In Calcutta, Shivaram and his partner were to perform with Neena Maya, who was trained in Russian ballet and performed in the theatres of China, Japan, Java, Burma and Malaya.⁶⁰ Neena's patron left for London and wrote back that he wouldn't be able to return to India soon. So, Neena requested the gentleman to organise a tour with Shivaram for her in London. Louise recalls,

> We began to arrange beautiful costumes for Shivaram's proposed appearances with her in London. A photographer called and took pictures of the pair in their Bharata Natya costumes.⁶¹

This proposed tour never eventuated, and because of a sudden cancellation on a cargo ship bound for Australia, Louise got a ticket to travel home, a chance she knew she might not get for another six-months.⁶² Onboard the ship, Louise thought of how Shivaram wept when she told him about her approaching journey. She also thought about Rajkumar Priyagopal Singh – a Manipuri dancer – who was planning to host Louise in Imphal, Manipur, with an ultimate motive to travel abroad with her as an impresario. Thinking aloud about these Hindu dancers and their yearning to showcase their talent abroad, Louise wrote,

> Oh, frustrated Indian dancers, born for the Creator Brahma's plan of showering righteousness to the world! Who in these times will help

you to fulfil your vocation? The boat's engine chugged away while my new role as a missionary of Hindu Art rose before me. The loved land of India was fading, while I saw as in a dream, my work, remembering to add the words "God Willing."[63]

Mary Louise Lightfoot notes that the journey back to Australia (May 1946), with this profound sense of purpose and dedication to Hindu dance, was the end of Louise's unpublished manuscript of her adventures.

In Melbourne, Louise successfully started preparing the public to receive her "treasure" – by publishing extensively on Hindu dance art in Australian newspapers and magazines, teaching selected Australian ballet students Indian dances and giving public talks at the Theosophical Society and ballet clubs.[64]

> Louise spoke of discovering Indian dance, an ancient and perfect art, though in danger of extinction; of Indian dance being more than entertainment, being considered an approach to God; and how the Hindu temple was the home of all arts.[65]

In addition, Mary Louise Lightfoot notes that Louise also started networking with people running art festivals and shows in Australia. Meanwhile, in India, Shivaram had left Neena Maya's troupe and joined Army Entertainment. As an entertainer for the troops, Shivaram performed in Singapore until the shipping routes were clear after the end of the war.[66]

In March 1947, Louise finally brought Shivaram to Australia and became his great publicist by painstakingly organising, publicising and explaining the art form to audiences through her well-researched lectures and commentaries. She, as planned, single-handedly controlled myriad other tasks associated with event management. Mary Louise Lightfoot recalls a conversation with Shivaram where he explained his first experience of landing in Melbourne:

> Shivaram's ship [*SS Marella*] sailed into Melbourne on the morning of March 20th 1947. The wharf seemed empty to him, compared to Indian wharves. Louise and Ruth met him at the pier, with some members of the press and a representative of the Australian-Indian Association. It was the first visit of an Indian dancer or artist to Australia. Up till then, no manager had been prepared to bring Uday Shankar's troupe to Australia, mostly because of the financial commitment needed, and because people were not at all accustomed to the music or dance of Asia.[67]

Shivaram arrived dressed in a grey *sherwani* (traditional Indian long coat), attracting the attention of the photojournalists eager to capture him. By the end of his visit, he was a star just like Louise dreamt of, in India. He was liked by everyone – the first Indian Kathakali artist to tour Australia (Figure 4.6).[68]

Shivaram, then in his early thirties, performed in all the major Australian cities: Melbourne, Sydney, Brisbane, Adelaide, Hobart and Perth. The Australian media overwhelmingly characterised him as an "exotic Hindu temple dancer." Whenever Lightfoot told his story to the audience, some

*Figure 4.6* (Left to right) Ananda Shivaram received by Louise Lightfoot at Port Melbourne on board *SS Marella*, 1947

Photographer: Unknown

Source: Photograph from the Louise Lightfoot Bequest, Monash University

Photograph Courtesy: Music Archives of Monash University and Mary Louise Lightfoot

ladies swooned: "That hair! Those eyes! And those TEETH! Oh! . . . profound."[69] Shivaram nonetheless found his visit labelled as a "unique" and "rare opportunity" from "the most expressive artist" of India.[70] In short, he was celebrated as a visiting cultural ambassador.

The promotional flyer for his very first program asserted boldly that Shivaram was a "famous and much travelled Hindu dancer" (Figure 4.7). For the Australian audiences, the flyer highlighted Shivaram's performances as

> a rare opportunity for those who cannot visit India to see some of the treasures hidden in remote villages of that country; exquisite hand-worked costumes and ornaments of ancient design, fantastic headdresses, beautiful designs of coloured make-up, dance techniques based on laws two thousand years old, acting by means of a special face-technique and gesture-language, the like of which is not found in any other part of the world.[71]

A journalist from the Australian newspaper the *Age* (April 29, 1947) helped to spread the word, declaring that,

> If you would fall under the spell of a brilliant Hindu dancer, Shivaram, and his company of European devotees, a visit to St. Peter's Eastern Hill this week should be well worthwhile. Dancing to Oriental music, Shivaram brought something to Melbourne last night which is a compound of beauty, mystic and transcendental symbolism and the ritual of the Brahmins in divertissements and the *Kathakali* dance drama.[72]

Shivaram's first major show was organised at the National Theatre in Melbourne, under the patronage of the Indian High Commissioner to Australia, Sir Raghunath Purushottam Paranjpye. The Indian media saw this collaboration between Shivaram, Lightfoot and other Australian Ballet artists as a much awaited "cultural union between the Orient and the Occident."[73] Artlover Madras, a pseudonym for a dance critic of the *Indian Express*, enthusiastically reported Shivaram's success:

> A new era has arisen and India has to take the lead in constructing union of the different races of the world. It is only by instilling an artistic sense into the minds of the masses that the mental outlook of nations can be broadened and in this great task Ananda Shivaram guided by his able and enlightened impresario has achieved a signal success.[74]

Artlover Madras was quick to add that even the dance critics of the Australian *Bulletin* felt the same way about Indian dance – "had there been

*Figure 4.7* Poster for Ananda Shivaram's first dance recital at the National Theatre, Melbourne, Victoria, April 28 to May 3, 1947

Photographer: Unknown

Source: Photograph from the Louise Lightfoot Bequest, Monash University

Photograph Courtesy: Music Archives of Monash University and Mary Louise Lightfoot

no White Australia, the Australian ballet would have progressed much by closer association with Hindustan."[75]

The *Argus* (April 29, 1947) first reported the initial practice and training sessions of the ballet *Indira Vijayam* at the National Theatre (Figure 4.8).

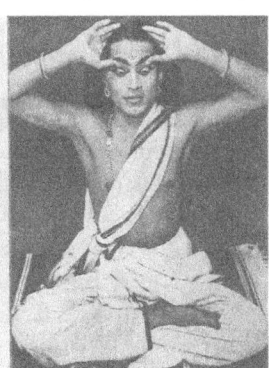

*Figure 4.8* Ananda Shivaram posing and performing eye exercises for Australian journalists, May 31, 1947

Photographer: *PIX* Magazine
Source: Photograph from the Louise Lightfoot Bequest, Monash University
Photograph Courtesy: Music Archives of Monash University and Mary Louise Lightfoot

Dressed as Lord Indra (the god of rain and lord of heaven in Hinduism), Shivaram commanded the journalist's attention:

> Students of the ballet and ballet enthusiasts generally will be interested in the performances of Indian dances which Shivaram, first Indian artist to visit Australia, is giving this week at the National Theatre ... Costumes and music add to the richness of the performances, but whether dancing the modern Indian style or the *Kathakali* – ancient Indian style – it is Shivaram who dominates everything. There is a graceful movement not only in his nimble feet, but also in his weaving arms and fingers, supple neck, and large, expressive eyes.[76]

The noted theatre and ballet critic Geoffrey Hutton, writing in the *Argus* (May 3, 1947), took obvious pleasure in Shivaram's performance. He observed that Indian dancing was not just "a museum piece" for students of art to appreciate, but rather any ballet lover would find "rare excitement" in Shivaram's "exquisite" performance.[77]

The extensive notes, commentaries, explanations and interpretation of the art of *Kathakali* that Lightfoot provided for the public came in as a "valuable aid." Drawing on her own experience, she made the "fascinating grace, spectacular beauty and historical charm" all plainly understandable.[78] Amazed by the hard work and time-consuming makeup technique, the correspondent of the *Sun Women's Magazine* (April 9, 1947) remarked that Shivaram had "brought most of the make-up components with him, and was

100  *The dancing God*

preparing them in the ancient Indian style by grinding colored stones with a pestle, and mixing them with coconut oil."[79]

As the tour proceeded, Lightfoot and Shivaram simplified the makeup by using flower-based colors for regular performances.[80] Since Kathakali is an art of word-tone drama performed in the open air, the costumes and makeup are bulky for dynamic characterisation. Makeup, characters grimaces and facial expressions are essential parts of Kathakali, especially in capturing the audiences. The character types in Kathakali are determined by the makeup; they are all named after it. There are seven basic kinds of makeup:

1  green (*pacca*)
2  ripe (*payuppu*)
3  knife (*katti*)
4  beard (*tati*)
5  black (*kari*)
6  radiant (*minukku*)
7  special (*teppu*)

Often heavy masks are used for select characters. Bharata describes four kinds of costumes and the graces along with different types of ornaments for actors and actresses. Gayanacharya Avinash C. Pandeya writes about the heavy, cumbersome and detailed costumes and makeup of Kathakali:

> The performer's entire body is swathed with over-flowing garments. An enormous skirt, somewhat resembling to women's costume of the Elizabethan period, is common to all male characters, except Brahmins and *risis*. Its bottom part is sufficiently wide and is provided with pleats. It hangs down below the knees. Underneath the outer skirt is a voluminous short skirt, something like a *tutu*. It gives wonderful swagger to the movements of an actor, who holds the skirt in a constant flare by the splayed position of his knees. The voluminous skirt is made of broad ribbons of white cotton embroidered cloth, interspersed with two or three red ones. It is tied round the waist in a way that free and dexterous movements are ensured. To either side of the skirt are attached embroidered cloth; in the front hangs *munti*, red flag decorated with crescents and stars. The body is covered with a coloured vest, over which many pieces of broad cloth, or strips, called *Uttarayan* and consisting of one red and several white pieces, hang from the neck. To two of these strips of cloth are attached to card-board, bell-shaped cups with mirrors, which are arrogantly manipulated by actors during, dance interludes. These are like a pair of the *manjras* (brass cymbals) commonly used in the dances of Tanjore and Manipur. The ends of these resemble inverted

lotuses. Heroes wear long-sleeved cotton jackets, short in size and red in colour (for, mostly, red matches the base colour of the make-up). A broad breast-plate and many garlands of beads cover the chest; metal epaulettes, the shoulders; and bracelets, the arms. The *Kotalaram* is the covering for the breast and made of some fine embroidered cloth.[81]

The greatest problem that Louise and Shivaram may have faced would be with regard to the chorus. Kathakali is usually a solo performance with only five or six characters in any play and no group dancing. To solve this, they divided the Kathakali dances into simple parts, so that it could be easily presented on the modern stage with live English commentary and original recordings of Kathakali music. As opposed to the Western theatre stage, the traditional stage is just a *Pandal*-like structure, that is decorated with green leaves and flowers and the space in the front of this is covered by mats for the audience.[82] The music used by Louise was the same as performed by orchestras from the temples of Kerala which incorporated the *manjira* (small cymbals), *chenda* (drum), *idakka* (hour-glass drum) and *shuddha madalam* (drum).

In relation to Shivaram and Louise's bold experiments in Kathakali, C. P. Unnikrishnan observes that Shivaram concentrated on the *nritya* (dance) aspect rather than the elaborate costumes or makeup.[83] For his international recitals, as can be seen in *Peacock Dance*, Shivaram was interested in delivering character-based emotions using well-designed body movements, without the use of cumbrous costumes and makeup. In her critically acclaimed Booker Prize-winning book – *The God of Small Things* – Arundhati Roy described why the artist never speaks about the story he is telling:

> To the Kathakali man, these stories are his children and his childhood. He has grown up within them. They are the house he was raised in, the meadows he played in. They are his windows and his way of seeing. So when he tells a story, he handles it as he would a child of his own. He teases it. He punishes it. He sends it up like a bubble. He wrestles it to the ground and lets it go again. He laughs at it because he loves it. He can fly you across whole worlds in minutes, he can stop for hours to examine a wilting leaf. Or play with a sleeping monkey's tail. He can turn effortlessly from the carnage of war into the felicity of a woman washing her hair in a mountain stream. From the crafty ebullience of a rakshasa with a new idea into a gossipy Malayali with a scandal to spread. From the sensuousness of a woman with a baby at her breast into the seductive mischief of Krishna's smile. He can reveal the nugget of sorrow that happiness contains. The hidden fish of shame in a sea of glory.[84]

102  *The dancing God*

Many sceptics considered these experimental dance-dramas as "unusual work for a classical ballet company."[85] However, others perceived the groundbreaking direction of the work as the collaborators had incorporated Kathakali dance into what previously had been a predominately European art form. In other words, Kathakali acted as "an invaluable asset" to the development of an "international art language – ballet."[86]

Lightfoot and Shivaram's experimentation in the fusion of Eastern and Western practices and making a classical Indian form accessible to uninitiated audiences, in this case, Australians, was an overwhelming success (Figure 4.9). A journalist from the *Western Australian* (January 12, 1950) lavished praise:

> The eloquence of gesture (even if its symbolism was not always understood), the flow of movement, the sure but often unobtrusive rhythm,

*Figure 4.9* Poster for Ananda Shivaram's dance recitals, 1947

Source: Photograph from the Louise Lightfoot Bequest, Monash University

Photograph Courtesy: Music Archives of Monash University and Mary Louise Lightfoot

the gorgeous costuming and the perfection of physical control could be at once appreciated. In all that was done, there was colour, poetry and form. Memories crowd in of the expressiveness of silver-pointed fingers, the flash of the eyes, the movement of bell-adorned ankles, of silhouettes on the backcloth. Yet it was when the element of mime was at its highest that the fullest appreciation was possible, and particularly, at least in the case of those uninitiated in Indian idioms, when there was the spoken word to help . . . it was more easily possible to comprehend the brilliant characterisations – of joy, fear, contemplation.[87]

Audiences and critics were bowled over by the eloquence, expressiveness and range of characterisation of Shivaram's Kathakali performances. After his first tour, Shivaram attracted attention from journalists and the public alike, in Australia, New Zealand and Fiji, as a picturesque figure with shoulder-length hair – a "short, slightly built man with flowing black hair, dressed in his national costume of all white."[88]

The critical consensus was that the audiences had viewed the ancient temple dances as if on a "magic carpet" ride.[89] The public was left amazed by Shivaram's exceptional "grace of movement, the subtlety of facial expression and aesthetic sensitivity together with an amazing simplicity of style."[90] His muscular control and facial expressions astounded the public:

> His eyes perform figures of eight in their sockets, revolve clockwise and anti-clockwise, and then one clockwise and the other anti-clockwise. Eyebrows, eyelashes, cheek and neck muscles all work overtime in the expression of mood, accompanying intricate gestures to an evolved rhythm.[91]

But beyond his refined technique, his imagination and vivid metamorphoses engaged spectators strongly. *Spotlight* magazine (1949) noted that in his performance, Shivaram took his audiences into "the realms of fantasy":

> We are the hermit awakening from his trance; the ferocious tiger, savage-eyed with bared teeth; we feel the grandeur of the surrounding mountains; see the trees grow in the rippling of his expressive arms; watch with his wondering eyes; the delicate beauty of his hands in the unfolding lotus bud. His outstanding charm lies in that mixture of masculine virility and serene inner spirituality.[92]

Previously unseen and now introduced by an obvious master of the form, Kathakali was embraced by attentive and enthusiastic audiences in Australia. Further, Shivaram's graceful dance movements were made easier to understand by Lightfoot's well-researched background commentaries and translations of the dance-dramas. These were often provided as short summaries through press releases and brochures that covered important aesthetic aspects and the cultural context of the Indian ballets. The audiences grasped the secrets of the gestural language and the intricacies of body movement and responded with standing ovations and unparalleled applause.

Soon, Shivaram was appearing alongside already established "brightly dressed musical ensembles" and in revues, such as *Stars and Garters* at the Majestic Theatre. In this revue, he joined comic Jimmy Wallace and musician John O'Connor to perform his colourful and exotic *Peacock Dance* (Figure 4.10).[93]

In spite of all the success on this journey, there was a price to pay. Within the four walls of a theatre and surrounded by friends and fans, Shivaram did not know that Australia, although a former colony of England, had its own racial prejudices towards Aborigines and Asians. On May 13, 1947, newspaper headlines read, "Dancer Refused Room; Slept in Theatre"[94] and "Shunned because of His Colour."[95] It shocked the entire art world in Australia, including Lightfoot, who had not imagined such prejudice would exist against a visiting artist.[96] Several attempts to obtain

*Figure 4.10* Ananda Shivaram in his iconic *Peacock Dance*, 1947
Photographer: John Tanner
Source: Photograph from the Louise Lightfoot Bequest, Monash University
Photograph Courtesy: Music Archives of Monash University and Mary Louise Lightfoot

a room for Shivaram by Lightfoot and others failed, as the "hotel and boarding-house proprietors objected to having an Indian as a guest."[97] The newspapers reported,

> Miss Louise Lightfoot, who brought [Shivaram] to Australia, said hotel accommodation in Adelaide was booked out so she had arranged for him to have a room in a boarding house. The landlady was willing to let the room *until she discovered his nationality*. Then she cancelled the booking, Miss Lightfoot said. Yesterday Shivaram still had nowhere to stay. Miss Lightfoot said she had found a lot of prejudice against India in Australia. She hoped Shivaram's demonstration of Indian art would be an education to Australians [emphasis my own].[98]

This news reached the Indian High Commission who telephoned to enquire about the whole incident. Louise played down the racial element of the incident and attributed it to a mere cultural misunderstanding caused by a promotional image (Figure 4.11). She clarified the Adelaide incident in her talk titled "A Few Stories of Shivaram by His Australian Impresario":

> Shivaram's first photographer, on hearing that he came from India, immediately requested "some savage expression." Shivaram showed the "Man-lion" face. The photo turned out to be really wonderful. We took it on to Adelaide, the next capital city. There we had great trouble in finding a hotel which would accept a "coloured" man; but towards the evening we found one. Next morning the hotel owner's wife came to me breathless. "He'll have to go! Look!" She showed the morning newspaper with the "Man-lion" picture. "Might frighten my children!" she said. Shivaram slept in the theatre foyer that night. The theatre manager passed the story to the Press. A "Whip-Cracker" artist from a vaudeville show in the same city offered Shivaram his room which he happened to be vacating; and the old widow there took a great fancy to Shivaram and came to see his show.[99]

Frank J. Martin, manager of the Tivoli Circuit, remarked in his press briefing that as an international artist, Shivaram was a cultural citizen of the world, and the "fact that an artist had a dark skin should not deprive him of amenities of civilisation."[100] When the people of Adelaide heard about the incident and read appeals in the newspapers, "more than 30 people rang the Majestic Theatre" and offered accommodation to Shivaram in their homes. Lightfoot soon made arrangements for Shivaram at the home of Mrs K. C. Teolar, an admirer of Shivaram's.[101] The *Canberra Times* followed this news and updated its readers: "Shivaram is now staying with a private family."[102]

106  *The dancing God*

*Figure 4.11* Ananda Shivaram in a Man-Lion pose from *Narasimha Avatar*, 1947
Photographer: The Advertiser
Source: Photograph from the Louise Lightfoot Bequest, Monash University
Photograph Courtesy: Music Archives of Monash University and Mary Louise Lightfoot

Shivaram, the victim of this racial prejudice, dismissed his "predicament with a smile and a shrug" in the press.[103] Shivaram, who felt "enchanted" to be in Australia and liked its weather, food and people, did not want to carry on any grudges. Many years later, he told Mary Louise Lightfoot that he was aware of the White Australia Policy but "didn't anticipate any problems. After all, people are always people."[104]

On his second tour of Australia in 1949, Shivaram's partner also performed.[105] Shivaram thanked the audiences and "spoke earnestly of friendship between the peoples of India and Australia."[106] Leaving behind the racist incident that happened earlier in Adelaide, he looked forward to a bright future: "My colour seems to have made no difference to the people here who are interested in the universal art of dancing."[107] For the Indian press, Shivaram's successful tour, the well wishes of his Australian friends and costars and the great ovations of "the White Australian" public forged, in themselves, "a momentous occasion" in history and the bilateral relations between the two countries. As they "seemed to have removed the stain of race prejudice from the Australian minds, at least during the one year he spent with them."[108]

In February 1948, Shivaram was booked to perform at the Repertory Theatre in Perth (Figure 4.12). The excitement can be gauged by the news report advertising his arrival:

> Shivaram is coming to Perth. In Sydney, Brisbane and Melbourne, the exotic dancer has captured the imagination of hundreds of theatregoers. When negotiations to bring him to Perth fell through it seemed that once again we were cut off from a great artist by that expensive barrier, the Nullarbor Plain. Enterprise, enthusiasm and hard work on the part of a few people have now assured that Shivaram will dance at the Repertory Theatre on February 14 and 16.[109]

Australian connoisseurs of ballet were "profoundly interested" and "pleasantly impressed" with Shivaram's "original demonstrations."[110] Comparing the dance style of Shivaram with that of the American modern dancer Ted Shawn, Seymour wrote in the *Mail*:

> Perhaps the most marvellous thing in Shivaram's dancing is his virility, which makes such a deep impression despite the fact that much of the Indian dancing is restrained, subtle, and extremely sensitive . . . [M]ale dancing is not the insipid, effeminate thing it has sometimes been thought, but . . . it unleashes before us a power and vitality completely masculine and astonishingly thrilling.[111]

Another example of Shivaram's success can be found in the Adult Education Board's Twenty-Second Summer School, held at the University of Western Australia in Perth (January 6–17, 1950). Highlighting its theme "The Australian Way of Life," this school program offered a line of star educators and orators as visiting tutors. But, in the midst of all the glitter of top academics and professional speakers, it turned out that Shivaram and his partner, who participated mainly in evening entertainments and recreational activities, became the chief attraction for Perth audiences and participants, with the summer school recording more than 350 enrollments that year.[112] Watched by large crowds at Winthrop Hall, their lectures and performances were thought by many admirers and art lovers to foster "cultural relations between India and the Commonwealth."[113]

An additional feather in Shivaram's cap was his performances in Tasmania (at Hobart, Launceston and Devonport) organised by the Adult Education

*Figure 4.12* Poster for Ananda Shivaram's dance recital at Repertory Theatre, Perth, Western Australia, 1948

Source: Photograph from the Louise Lightfoot Bequest, Monash University

Photograph Courtesy: Music Archives of Monash University and Mary Louise Lightfoot

Board. In the *Mercury* (March 31, 1950), Minerva reported the enthusiasm and excitement among the theatregoers:

> Tasmania has been overlooked many times in the itinerary of famous dancers on tour in Australia, and it is hoped that full support will be accorded to the recitals to be given at the Playhouse, Hobart on Wednesday and Thursday next, by the world-renowned Indian dancer.[114]

The *Advocate* (April 19, 1950) called his Tasmanian tour an "outstanding success," which "proved that the Tasmanian public is interested in more such cultural programmes" and exchanges between India and Australia.[115] At one point, a teenage variety dancer, having a free view of Shivaram's *Kamadeva* (Love God) from backstage, turned to Lightfoot and exclaimed, "Oh Gawd! I could go on watchin' 'im forever!"[116] To many Australian journalists, Shivaram came across as a good-natured Indian with a great sense of humour, particularly in his habit of taking English-language idioms literally. During Shivaram's visit to South Australia, Walter Desborough, one of the pioneers of ballet in Australia, invited him to lecture and demonstrate to his students. The *Mail* (May 31, 1947) reported in "Round Town," Shivaram's exchanges with Desborough and his pupils:

> "May I take your coat," said Desborough when the Indian called.
> "Certainly," said Shivaram bewildered, "but it may be too small."[117]

And,

> "How do you like your tea?"
> "Very much, indeed," said Shivaram.[118]

Much later, Shivaram acknowledged to a journalist of the *Sunday Times* (January 8, 1950) in Perth, "I speak your English very bad."[119] However, the language barrier did not diminish Shivaram's popularity in Australia. In his column "Out among the People" in the *Advertiser* (June 11, 1947), Vox called Shivaram a "planet" surrounded by fans and well-wishers, after the cashier of a well-known city restaurant where Shivaram was dining predicted to her friends that the race-horse named "Star of India" would win the next day at the races – and it did (Figure 4.13).[120] Shivaram, the "star of India" and a winner in another realm, enjoyed constant attention from an excited public. Some Australian dance teachers and keen students of Indian philosophy and dance, like Mrs Minnie Salear, Mrs Wilfred Thomas and Mrs K. C. Teolar, even followed Shivaram throughout his recitals in every state in Australia. Thousands of people came to see his performances, and

*Figure 4.13* Ananda Shivaram in *Ras Leela*, ca. 1940–1947
Photographer: Unknown
Source: https://trove.nla.gov.au/version/13120467. Call No. PIC/8801 LOC Box PIC/8801
Photograph Courtesy: National Library of Australia, Canberra

critics noted key reasons for the success of Shivaram's tour: "the simplicity, emotional intensity, grace and strength of this superb artist."[121]

Shivaram's first impressions of Australia and its people (especially women) were recorded by the *Sun Women's Magazine* (April 9, 1947) in an exclusive interview: "Australian people are very friendly" but "women carry themselves badly."[122] Shivaram, who himself walked with "the lithe grace of a panther" noticed that Australian girls "are a little stiff, a little as if they are a machine wound to make them go."[123] He was a guest of honour at many social gatherings. He gave lectures, demonstrations, radio talks, and press interviews and trained schoolchildren and young ballet artists interested in Kathakali.

Just like Uday Shankar, who, in the 1930s, was surrounded by a female audience, Shivaram too had his own female patronage.[124] To the Australian public, Shivaram appeared to be a young, successful and ever-smiling Indian folkloric hero, followed by

> the usual bevvy of women who sighed rapturously every time the dancer lifted his little finger and exclaimed loudly at his merest wriggle in the hope that they would be mistaken for experts. "What grace." "What fluidity of movement." And so on.[125]

Hiding behind Shivaram's laughter and beautiful smile was a painful truth that he told to the *Australian Women's Weekly* (April 15, 1950).[126] Although he belonged to a family of temple dancers, born and bred in the tradition, and knew of "no other life" than dancing, even he had to painfully convince his mother and her relatives that he wanted dancing as his occupation.[127] Shivaram's father, Gopala Panicker, had been a failure as the breadwinner for the family and ultimately had to turn to work on the farm or paddy fields of the local landlord to support his family. Louise observed in relation to his life's work that Guru Panicker was "utterly devoted to the great but poorly paid art" and "longing for a perfect troupe he almost reduced his family to poverty."[128] In 1941, during a visit to his home, Shivaram bitterly explained his family's financial position to Louise: "He is taking round a Kathakali troupe not a first class one. For two years he had troupe of the best actors that is how we became poor."[129] Now a huge international success and a major economic contributor toward his household, Shivaram felt grateful to Lightfoot for saving him from an impending future in which "he would be suffering scolding from his mother, and uncles, and aunts for idling his time away as a five-rupees-a-week temple dancer, after he had completed his twelve years' gruelling course as a Kathakali dancer."[130] Mary Louise Lightfoot notes that from the proceeds of his Australian tours, Shivaram was able to build a two-storey house in his village.[131]

Shivaram was on his way to becoming an international star. A rich Indian-origin businessman invited Louise and Shivaram to Fiji, and they were "put up" at the iconic Grand Pacific Hotel (Figure 4.14).[132] On their return to Melbourne, Louise and Shivaram were told by the officers of the immigration department that Shivaram's visa was meant for Australia and his Fiji tour had led to its cancellation. On Louise's request, the officials granted a few weeks' of stay to Shivaram to make arrangements for his travel back to India. But Shivaram was now ready to move on and explore Europe. Mary

*Figure 4.14* (Sitting in the centre, from left to right) Ruth Bergner, Ananda Shivaram and Louise Lightfoot, Fiji, 1950

Photographer: Unknown
Source: Photograph from the Louise Lightfoot Bequest, Monash University
Photograph Courtesy: Music Archives of Monash University and Mary Louise Lightfoot

Louise Lightfoot notes that Louise and Shivaram boarded *Marseilles* from the port of Freemantle bound for Ceylon and Bombay. They did not get down at Bombay as planned and moved on to London to showcase India's new cultural ambassador – "Instead of returning then to India, something told me to go to London. A crazy and expensive venture perhaps."[133]

From 1947–1950, Shivaram performed in Australia, Fiji, New Zealand and England with Louise as his trusted impresario.[134] He mesmerised and enchanted his Australian audiences with awe-inspiring performances of the following dances:

- *Runga Pooja* – a sacred dance in praise of the presiding deity of the stage, offering salutations to the audiences
- *Kamadeva* – a cupid dance about Lord Shiva and Parvathi's love
- *The Hermit* – the story of the great Indian sage and writer Kalidasa
- *Ras Leela* – a dance expressing the legendary love story of Lord Krishna and his beloved Radha

- *Peacock Dance* – a dance portraying the peacock's joy in seeing the approaching monsoon
- *Indra Vijayam* – a dance about Lord Indra, god of the heavens, and his fight over mighty mountains
- *King Rugmangadan* – the story of a king's triumph over temptations sent to test his devotion by the Lord Vishnu

In the 1950s, Shivaram wanted to rest after years of touring continuously, and Louise was interested in learning other traditional dance forms of India, especially Manipur.[135] This holiday was her chance to learn and popularise a form older than the Kathakali – the Hindu dances of Manipur.

## Notes

1 Parts of this chapter have appeared as "Staging a Cultural Collaboration: Louise Lightfoot and Ananda Shivaram's First Indian Dance Tour of Australia, 1947–1949" in *Dance Chronicle* 38, no. 3 (2015): 305–35. Published here with the permission of Taylor and Francis.
2 Lightfoot, *Lightfoot Dancing*, Chapter 12.
3 Ibid.
4 Ibid.
5 Ibid., Chapter 13.
6 Madhavan has worked with Uday Shankar and was bringing Western ideas of dancing, particularly having a key female partner, on stage. Later, he was dismissed as a teacher from Kerala Kalamandalam for misconduct. See Lightfoot, *Lightfoot Dancing*, Chapter 14.
7 Ibid.
8 See Bapat, *Re-scribing Tradition*, 61; Zarilli, *The Kathakali Complex*, 51.
9 Lightfoot, *Lightfoot Dancing*, Chapter 21.
10 Seymour, "Presenting Louise Lightfoot," 51.
11 Lightfoot, *Lightfoot Dancing*, Chapter 14.
12 Seymour, "Presenting Louise Lightfoot," 51. The great god – *Mahadeva* – Lord Shiva, the cosmic dancer or *yogi* who is also the preserver and destroyer in Hindu religion, is considered Lord of Dance – *Nataraj*. See Coomaraswamy, *The Dance of Shiva*, 1975.
13 Lightfoot, "Explanation of Items by Miss Lightfoot's Hindu Dance Group," 1947b.
14 For globalisation of local Malabar ritual practices, see Tarabout, "Malabar Gods, Nation-building and World Culture," 2005.
15 Lightfoot, "Explanation of Items by Miss Lightfoot's Hindu Dance Group," 1947b.
16 Unnikrishnan, "Ananda Shivaram Bids Farewell to the Aesthetic World," 2001.
17 Lightfoot, *Lightfoot Dancing*, Chapter 14.
18 Seymour, "Presenting Louise Lightfoot," 51.
19 "His English Is 'Very Bad' but His Dancing Is Good," 8.
20 For a discussion on state patronage to Indian dance forms, see Shah, "State Patronage in India," 2002.
21 Coorlawala, "Ruth St. Denis and India's Dance Renaissance," 148.
22 Ibid., 147–48.
23 Lightfoot, *Lightfoot Dancing*, Chapter 14.
24 Ibid., Chapter 15.

25 For a discussion of experimentation in Kathakali, see Fischer-Lichte, *Dionysus Resurrected*, 2013; Zarrilli, *Kathakali Dance Drama*, 2000.
26 Ram Gopal published two books, see Gopal and Dadachanji, *Indian Dancing*, 1951; Gopal, *Rhythms in the Heavens*, 1957.
27 See Venkataraman, "Ambassador of Indian Dance," 2003.
28 Ibid.
29 Lightfoot, *Lightfoot Dancing*, Chapter 15.
30 Ibid.
31 Ibid.
32 Ibid., Chapter 16.
33 Despite the extraordinary reach and patronage offered by well-known artists, writers and political figures, such as Michael Chekhov, John Martin, Pundit Jawaharlal Nehru, Romain Rolland, Sir William Rothenstein, Leopold Stokowski, and Rabindranath Tagore, Shankar's Centre lasted only four years. See Vertinsky and Ramachandran. "Uday Shankar and the Dartington Hall Trust," 298.
34 Ibid., Chapter 17.
35 Ibid.
36 Ibid.
37 For more details, see Kumar, "Meet Sujata and Asoka, the Indo-German Dancers Who Charmed Hollywood in the 1950s," 2016.
38 Ibid., Chapter 18.
39 Ibid.
40 Ibid., Chapter 19.
41 Ibid., Chapter 18.
42 Ibid., Chapter 19.
43 Ibid., Chapter 20.
44 Ibid.
45 Ibid.
46 Ibid.
47 Ibid.
48 Ibid., Chapter 21.
49 Ibid.
50 Ibid.
51 Ibid., Chapter 22.
52 Ibid., Chapter 23.
53 Ibid.
54 Ibid.
55 Ibid., Chapter 24.
56 Ibid., Chapter 25.
57 See Lightfoot, "A Few Stories of Shivaram by His Australian Impresario," 1947a.
58 Lightfoot, *Lightfoot Dancing*, Chapter 25.
59 Ibid.
60 Ibid.
61 Ibid.
62 Ibid.
63 Ibid.
64 See Sarwal, *Louise Lightfoot in Search of India*, 2017; Lightfoot, *Lightfoot Dancing*, Chapter 26.
65 Ibid.
66 Ibid.

67 Ibid.
68 See "Hindu Dancer Astounds with Muscle Control," 1950; Artlover Madras, "Ananda Shivaram: India's Cultural Ambassador," 3; Broinowski, *The Yellow Lady*, 1996.
69 Lightfoot, "A Few Stories of Shivaram by His Australian Impresario," 1947a.
70 "Shivaram Here on December 9th," 1949.
71 "National Theatre Movement of Australia," 1947.
72 "Hindu Dance Artist: Symbolism and Beauty," 1947.
73 Artlover Madras, "Ananda Shivaram: India's Cultural Ambassador," 3.
74 Ibid.
75 Ibid.
76 "Indian Dancer Impressive," 1947.
77 Hutton, "Toward a Theatre; New Plays and Big Names Coming," 1947, 17.
78 "Indian Dancer: Entrancing Display by Shivaram," 10.
79 "Friendly Indian Likes Us," 1947.
80 The materials that comprise traditional *Kathakali* makeup are obtained from natural substances: *chenchilyam* powder and coconut oil (basic facial); mix of rice flour and lime (white); vermillion or red earth (red); *manayola* mineral (yellow); powdered mix of *manayola* mineral and sapphire (blue); and gingelly oil's soot or *kajal* (black).
81 Pandeya, *The Art of Kathakali*, 125–26.
82 Ibid., 134.
83 Unnikrishnan, "Ananda Shivaram Bids Farewell to the Aesthetic World," 2001.
84 Roy, *The God of Small Things*, 230–31.
85 Brissenden and Glennon, *Australia Dances*, 84.
86 Lightfoot, "Two Thousand Years of Rhythm," 16; See also "Tale of a Peacock Tail Picture," 8.
87 "Dances of India: Colour and Poetry at University," 1950.
88 "Temple Dancer Says Fiji an Indian's Paradise," 4.
89 "Dancers' Art Delights," 1950.
90 "Indian Dances by Master," 1947.
91 "Hindu Dancer Astounds with Muscle Control," 1950.
92 Wilkinson, "The Return of Shivaram," 1949.
93 "Three New Acts at Majestic: Indian Dancer in Bright Revue," 1947.
94 "Dancer Refused Room," 2.
95 "Shunned Because of His Colour," 1947.
96 "Accommodation for Indian Dancer," 3.
97 "Many Offer Lodgings for Indian," 1947.
98 "Dancer Refused Room," 2.
99 Lightfoot, "A Few Stories of Shivaram by His Australian Impresario," 1947a.
100 "Many Offer Lodgings for Indian," 1947.
101 "The Life of Melbourne," 1947.
102 "Accommodation for Indian Dancer," 3.
103 "Dancer Refused Room," 2.
104 Lightfoot, *Lightfoot Dancing*, Chapter 26.
105 "First Woman Dancer from India Reaches Perth," 1950.
106 "Malayalam," 1950.
107 Ibid.
108 Artlover Madras, "Ananda Shivaram: India's Cultural Ambassador," 3.
109 Seymour, "Presenting Louise Lightfoot," 51.

110 "Indian Dancer: Entrancing Display by Shivaram," 10.
111 Seymour, "Presenting Louise Lightfoot," 51.
112 "Record Enrolments for Summer School," 1950.
113 "Need for a New Type of School Teacher," 1950.
114 Minerva, "Theatre Royal Begins New Page in Its History Tonight," 22.
115 "Indian Dancer Pleases Big Devonport Audience," 1950.
116 Lightfoot, "A Few Stories of Shivaram by His Australian Impresario," 1947a.
117 "Shivaram," 1947.
118 Ibid.
119 "His English Is 'Very Bad' but His Dancing Is Good," 8.
120 Vox, "He Is a Planet Now," 1947.
121 Seymour, "Presenting Louise Lightfoot," 51.
122 "Friendly Indian Likes Us," 1947.
123 Ibid.
124 See Vertinsky and Ramachandran, "Uday Shankar and the Dartington Hall Trust," 41.
125 "Tale of a Peacock Tail Picture," 8.
126 "Temple Dancing Runs in Family," 21.
127 "Tale of a Peacock Tail Picture," 8.
128 Lightfoot, *Lightfoot Dancing*, Chapter 21.
129 Ibid.
130 "Temple Dancing Runs in Family," 21.
131 Lightfoot, *Lightfoot Dancing*, Chapter 26.
132 Ibid.
133 Ibid.
134 As Louise's friendship and respect for Shivaram's work grew, she focused particularly on arranging performances for Shivaram (1947, Australia; 1948, London and Fiji; 1949, Australia and New Zealand; 1952, Japan; 1953, Canada; 1954, 1955, and 1960–1963, U.S.; 1957, Australia and Indonesia; 1959 and 1963–1967, Canada; 1974, Australia).
135 Lightfoot, *Lightfoot Dancing*, Chapter 28.

# Conclusion
## Temple dreaming[1]

In 1951, the Indian Government Trade Commissioner's office commended Louise Lightfoot's passion for promoting Indian dance abroad. They noted, "Her ambition and mission in life is cultural revival of India and propagation of this art abroad. She has made untiring efforts to spread this cultural message in Australia and New Zealand."[2] It has been a great challenge for a traditional Hindu dancer, especially Kathakali, to tamper with the age-old tradition.[3] However, Louise, along with Shivaram, successfully achieved her goals. In this endeavour, she was supported by an ensemble of Australian dancers, including Misha Burlakov, Ruth Bergner, Moya Beaver, Leona Welch, Pat Martin and Betty Russell. They toured and promoted a range of Indian classical dance forms, such as Kathakali, Manipuri, Bharatanatyam, Kathak, Kuchipudi, Odissi, Chhau and Mohiniyattam throughout India, Ceylon, Australia, England, New Zealand, Fiji, Japan, the United States and Canada. Like many modern cross-cultural collaborations, these dancers too were interested in presenting the traditional Hindu dances alongside contemporary choreographies beyond the boundaries of India.

The Australian tours were made possible by the generous official assistance of state funding bodies, such as the Arts Council of Australia, the Adult Education Board (in Western Australia and in Tasmania) and the Council of Adult Education (in Victoria). The Indian dancers performed at prestigious theatres, such as the National Theatre in Melbourne, the Majestic Theatre in Adelaide and the Repertory Theatre in Perth.

In 1949, after his successful first Australian tour, the *Indian Express* (June 6, 1949) hailed him as the true "cultural ambassador" of India in Australia.[4] Shivaram interacted with both Australian artists and the common people to promote knowledge of his art and to bring Indian and Australian cultures and worlds closer together. His performances also resulted in a period of vitality in the Australian dance scene, stemming from an exposure to Indian dance forms. Shivaram became a popular personality and cast a profound impression on many, through his presentations of Kathakali.[5]

118  *Conclusion*

He also taught Kathakali and the art of experimental fusion (of Eastern and Western dance forms) to young Australian students and ballet dancers (Figure 5.1). His tours, lectures, and demonstrations of Indian dance held "great cultural significance," as they "enhanced the respect of Whites of Australia for the intellectual heritage of India."[6] While Shivaram's experimental presentations of Kathakali received applause and rave reviews in the West, Unnikrishnan observes that Indian and South Asian audiences often objected that in his modern interpretations, he had sacrificed the classical Indian tradition.[7] As an artist, Shivaram remained true to his art and vision in making Kathakali accessible to wider audiences, both in the East and in the West, marking his capability of being ahead of his time. Moreover, his unique experimentation left a stylistic mark on many ballet artists and choreographers in Australia, such as Walter Desborough (*Indian Harvest Dance*, 1949) and Anita Ardell (*Indo-Jazz Suite*, 1967), who followed his work closely for inspiration.

*Figure 5.1* Shivarim [i.e.] Shivaram fans out his peacock plumage in an impromptu demonstration of Kathakali to Australian schoolchildren, 1974

Photograph: John Tanner for the Australian Information Service
Source: https://trove.nla.gov.au/version/20004873. Call No. PIC BOX PIC/8915 #PIC/8915/2
Photograph Courtesy: National Library of Australia, Canberra

## Conclusion    119

During the 1960s, some of Louise and Shivaram's main artistic work continued in San Francisco (USA). The duo educated the American public to appreciate Indian dance and eventually taught it to hundreds of students. Shivaram settled down in the United States and started a dance school in partnership with Louise to promote Kathakali through lecture-demonstrations in American and Canadian universities and galleries. Further, to keep his global dance connections active in Kerala, Shivaram started an institution dedicated to classical dances called the See India Foundation in Cochin (Kerala). This also housed the first daily tourist theatre for Kathakali. According to P. K. Devan, Shivaram's youngest brother and director of the Foundation, "the institute leads the visitors through Kathakali to the ever-updated ethos of Indian concepts of spirituality and philosophy" that Shivaram strived to propagate.[8] Decades of hard work and dedication to Kathakali earned Shivaram the Kerala Sangeetha Nataka Akademi Fellowship and a visiting professorship at San Francisco University. In 1974 and 1976, Shivaram returned to give his final performance at Monash University with Malaysian-born Australian dancer Chandrabhanu and Australian modern dancer Ruth Bergner. On November 7, 2001, at the age of eighty-six, this daring experimenter, whose subtle expression of emotions spellbound millions of dance connoisseurs in India and abroad, left for his eternal abode in his village, Ezhikkara, near Cochin.

Building on the project that Poet Vallathol started in the 1920s, Shivaram succeeded in promoting Kathakali at both national and international levels by gaining recognition for himself as a global cultural citizen and for Kathakali as a classical art among "the world's great classical arts."[9]

Louise lived and worked at the yoga ashram of Swami Vishnudevananda in Montreal, Canada (Figure 5.2 and Figure 5.3).[10] In 1967, she returned to Melbourne and lived a simple life. Louise never married and finally retired in 1968. Mary Louise Lightfoot notes that Louise wanted to retire in "a cottage with a cat and geraniums, somewhere north of Sydney."[11] Even in her retirement, Louise stayed actively involved in multicultural dance performances and festivals, especially at Monash University's Department of Music.[12] At Monash, she worked closely with Australia-based Indian dancers, presenting dancers from India and leading the way for multicultural dance traditions and expressions to find a place in Australian imagination (Figure 5.4).[13] Louise became ill with pneumonia, and she died on May 18, 1979, at Malvern. She was buried in the Cheltenham cemetery. Louise's sister Lal told Mary Louise Lightfoot,

> Her last years were not very happy ones. She spent a lot of time in the hospital, which did not please her or suit her at all. As fast as she recovered from one thing, another happened. Mais had to keep her contented

*Figure 5.2* (Left and centre) Louise Lightfoot and Yamini Krishnamurti at Swami Vishnudevananda's ashram near Montreal

Photographer: Unknown

Source: Photograph from the Louise Lightfoot Bequest, Monash University

Photograph Courtesy: Music Archives of Monash University and Mary Louise Lightfoot

in Oakleigh after being all around the world. It was very much a narrowing of interests. Though she kept up her interest in music, dancing and singing, she was not able to do much.[14]

The *Indian Express* (July 2, 1979) lamented the death of "Kathakali's Australian mother." To me, Louise's life work in Australia was very similar to one of her American contemporaries, Stella Kramrisch. Prof. Kramrisch's contribution to the study, teaching and popularising of Hindu art in the United States is well-known, and in 1982, the Indian government even awarded her with the highest civilian award, the Padma Bhushan.[15] Sadly, no such accolade or recognition has come Louise's way from either the Indian or the Australian government, posthumously.[16]

As noted earlier, before her death, Louise donated boxes filled with her writings, books, dance compositions, audio material, notes on music and press clippings of her tours with Indian artists to the Music Archives at Monash University. In 1996, using some of the material from the music archives,

Conclusion 121

*Figure 5.3* (Third from right) Louise Lightfoot with a Kathakali troupe from Kerala at Swami Vishnudevananda's ashram near Montreal

Photographer: Unknown

Source: Photograph from the Louise Lightfoot Bequest, Monash University

Photograph Courtesy: Music Archives of Monash University and Mary Louise Lightfoot

renowned Indian-Australian dancer and choreographer Tara Rajkumar, OAM, created a dance and "dialogic performance" entitled *Temple Dreaming* (Figure 5.5).[17] This dance drama revived the memory of Louise Lightfoot and her passion for Kathakali.

*Temple Dreaming* was first performed in Australia at the Alexander Theatre at Monash University and later toured India. Tara observed that in this dance project, she "moved from a strictly theatrical tradition of solo performance into an ensemble work and creating symbols totally new to the particular dance tradition."[18] This was a unique project created with the help of several Australian dancers and juxtaposed both the traditional and contemporary Western and Indian dancing styles. According to Tara, it acknowledged through performance Louise's contribution to the Australia-Indian dance scene: "Her symbolic association with India and her classical dance forms, particularly Kathakali, became the highlight for me and the focal point for the production."[19] Just like my experience, for Tara too, Louise's personal documentation was a fascinating discovery "of a meeting between

*Figure 5.4* Louise Lightfoot, 1978
Photographer: Unknown
Source: Photograph from the Louise Lightfoot Bequest, Monash University
Photograph Courtesy: Music Archives of Monash University and Mary Louise Lightfoot

vastly different dance traditions and styles."[20] In an interview with Dr Sunil Kothari, she observes,

> Until I opened the trunk stored in the archives of Monash University's Music department all those years ago, Louise Lightfoot had been nothing more than a name to me. But once I began delving through its contents – the diaries, papers and artistic mementoes – the spell was cast. I was so inspired by what I discovered from Lightfoot's mementoes that I created a dance theatre show about the life of this fascinating Australian expatriate.[21]

*Figure 5.5* Mary Louise Lightfoot; Dr Sunil Kothari; Tara Rajkumar, OAM; and Chandralekha at the performance of *Temple Dreaming* in Chennai, India, 1997

Photograph Courtesy: Tara Rajkumar, OAM, and Mary Louise Lightfoot

The Louise Lightfoot Collection of the Monash University Music Archives inspired her to create this performance project.

> Each object that I looked at, each box that I opened, brought back memories of my training in Kerala, the southernmost state of India, and the powerful images of life and performance which had gripped me as a student learning Kathakali. Equally engrossing and personally involving were Lightfoot's biographical notes. There were so many points of contact that I identified with – people, places and references which belonged to my childhood's storehouse of memories.[22]

For Tara, creating a dance performance on Louise's life in India and her contribution to Hindu temple dance became a challenge. She writes,

> How do I put across these closely shared references to an Australian audience of today which has very little association with any of these significant performance factors? How do I realise some of the

excitement that Kathakali and the Temple Dances aroused in Lightfoot and captured her imagination? As I delved into her writings and records of her journeys, my journey into creating a performance started to assume a definite course.[23]

As she delved deeper into Louise's notes and drafted her own ideas about the performance project, Tara realised a few similarities about Louise and herself. She writes,

> Being primarily a performer, I realised that Louise Lightfoot and I were fascinated by the same performance idiom and vocabulary. She was not a dancer and her ego was not that of a performer. In fact, she revelled in communicating this Eastern dance tradition, which she had discovered, to a totally alien and uninitiated Western audience. She wanted to take to the rest of the world the beauty and perfection she perceived in Kathakali when she arrived in Kerala. For me, this intense dedication and intrinsic love of a dance form, a performance idiom, a theatre tradition, became the common factor between the subject of my research and myself. I was born to it; she revived and pursued it with a passion.[24]

Now, it was crucial for Tara to capture and re-create the Kathakali dance form for the audiences as faithfully as possible to the one originally seen by Louise in the villages of Kerala in the 1930s. The logic behind this was to use the dance theatre tradition and take the audience through a journey of discovery.[25] To achieve this, Tara created specific imagery and selected objects from the archives that can transport the audiences to Louise's first impressions of India. She writes,

> For example, a large metal box (trunk) found in the Louise Lightfoot Music Archives became an essential part of the performance. In it was a big chunk of the special life of Lightfoot which was turning into performance. The trunk, therefore, became symbolic of discovery. Contrary to traditional performances, *Temple Dreaming* began in the theatre foyer with a sculptural installation being signified with activated sound and light effects. The trunk became the base for the installation from which rose a figure capturing a fragment of the essence of the Dance of Siva, the dance that attracted Louise Lightfoot to India.[26]

The scenes were further helped by an activated voice that projected Louise's words from her journal explaining her immense love for India and Hindu temple dance.

As audiences move further into *Temple Dreaming*, they are face to face with Tara. Her own story and the discovery of Louise Lightfoot's collection is also part of the performance. She notes that the last scene of the performance reflects the arrival of dancers like herself into Australia. This not only highlights the changing nature of dance audiences and the art forms but also establishes a dance dialogue that suggests continuity.[27] Tara observes,

> Lightfoot brought Kathakali as an alien art form, as exotica. Its presence today gives it a transmigrant quality and status. Here I begin to validate its existence as a performance idiom with the potential for socially persuasive performance practice. In other words, it has the potential for contemporary development.[28]

To create *Temple Dreaming*, Tara involved the members of the Natya Sudha Dance Company, a multicultural group (Figure 5.6). According to her,

*Figure 5.6* A scene from *Temple Dreaming* choreographed by Tara Rajkumar, OAM, India, 1997

Photograph Courtesy: Tara Rajkumar, OAM

multicultural dance in Australia has given rise to a more eclectic approach to classical dance in the West.

> In the case of South Asian performance tradition although still in a state of transition, some clear possibilities for effective contemporary performance are gradually evolving and invite a greater and more in-depth analysis and inquiry. I encapsulate my inquiry thus far in the last scene of *Temple Dreaming* by making the dance movements a symbolic embodiment of the discovery of a sacred space by each dancer in a new environment.[29]

Thanks to Louise Lightfoot's pioneering spirit and dedication to Indian dance, the Indian subcontinent's classical dance in different styles is now regularly staged in various Australian cities by a number of resident multicultural dance companies along with ballet and contemporary dance. It would be right to say that dance in Australia has been shaped by her influence and ground-breaking work.

Today, Indian dance in Australia is celebrated and represented by professional dance artists, companies, schools and amateur community groups. These have, over the years, performed traditional Indian classical dances, Bhangra and Bollywood in various cultural festivals organised throughout Australia. Lightfoot's collaboration with Shivaram gave Australian audiences this exposure to Indian dance. Their dance tours had "great cultural significance," and these dance performances, lectures and demonstrations "considerably enhanced the respect of Whites of Australia for the intellectual heritage of India."[30] Noticing the unfailing excitement among Australian audiences, the Arts Council also extended financial support to similar dance recitals subsequently. Shivaram's impact and profound impression on many Australian dancers through Kathakali is acknowledged even today – something that even Louise did not expect to accomplish.[31] Shivaram, who moved in the social life of Australia and charmed journalists and audiences alike, brought the two cultures closer and stimulated a period of vitality and originality through Indian dance form.

In conclusion, over and above curiosity, it must have been difficult, both aesthetically and artistically, for Australian audiences to understand and fully appreciate Hindu dance form with its roots in a tradition reaching back to 3000 BC. As an early image-maker in both pre- and post-independent India, Shivaram, with the help of Louise, de-provincialised and popularised Hindu dances in the international dance circuit. They organised this unique space in the utopian dream for multicultural dance and the arts that paved the way for other Indian dancers and troupes.[32] These notably included Rajkumar Priyagopal Singh, Ibetombi Devi, Tilakavati, Indrani, Bhaskar, the

Chitrasena Ballet, Song and Dance Theatre, Kalakshetra, Kerala Kalamandalam, Balagopalam, Masked Dancers of Bengal, V. Gayatri, Krishnaveni Lakshmanan, Yamini Krishnamurti, Vyajayanthimala, Daksha Sheth, Jyotikana Ray, Mallika Sarabhai, Sonal Mansingh, Birju Maharaj, Sanjukta Panigrahi, Bimbavati Devi, Guru Banamali Sinha, Sruti Bandopadhay and many others. Over the years, they have come to participate in various dance and cultural festivals organised throughout Australia. It is my hope that this book will contribute not only to our understanding of the Hindu dance or Indian classical dance's arrival in Australia but also to our deeper understanding of other historical and contemporary cross-cultural connections of a transnational nature between the two countries.

## Notes

1 I am grateful to Tara Rajkumar, OAM, for sharing her paper, "The Fragile Gesture," which helped me in shaping the story behind her dance performance *Temple Dreaming* (1996).
2 Lightfoot, *Lightfoot Dancing*, Chapter 29.
3 Kothari, "New Directions in Indian Dance," 2008; Fischer-Lichte, *Dionysus Resurrected*, 2013.
4 Artlover Madras, "Ananda Shivaram: India's Cultural Ambassador," 3.
5 Shaw, "Currently Narrating 'Kathakali' in Montreal," 1959.
6 Artlover Madras, "Ananda Shivaram: India's Cultural Ambassador," 3.
7 Unnikrishnan, "Ananda Shivaram Bids Farewell to the Aesthetic World," 2001.
8 Ibid.
9 Zarrilli, *Kathakali Dance Drama*, 31.
10 Vishnudevananda Saraswati was founder of the International Sivananda Yoga Vedanta Centres and Ashrams. He established the Sivananda Yoga Teachers' Training Course, one of the first yoga teacher training programs in the West.
11 Lightfoot, *Lightfoot Dancing*, Chapter 36.
12 Lightfoot, "Lightfoot, Louise," 2008.
13 At Monash University, Louise Lightfoot successfully organised shows and workshops for Shivaram (1974 and 1976) and Sonal Mansingh (1976).
14 Lightfoot, *Lightfoot Dancing*, Chapter 36.
15 See Miller, *Exploring India's Sacred Art*, 1983.
16 "Australian *Kathakali* Artiste Dead," 1979.
17 Tara Rajkumar, OAM, an accomplished Indian Mohiniattam and Kathakali dancer, was conferred with the Medal of Order of Australia in 2009 for her contribution to multiculturalism and arts in Australia.
18 Rajkumar, "Fragile Gesture," 36.
19 Ibid.
20 Ibid.
21 Kothari, "Australian Diary: Part 2," 2009.
22 Rajkumar, "Fragile Gesture," 36.
23 Ibid.
24 Ibid., 36–37.
25 Ibid., 37.

26 Ibid.
27 Ibid.
28 Ibid.
29 Ibid., 38.
30 Artlover Madras, "Ananda Shivaram: India's Cultural Ambassador," 3.
31 Shaw, "Currently Narrating 'Kathakali' in Montreal," 1959.
32 For a detailed discussion of Indian dancers and capital pulls of the global stage, see Srinivasan, *Sweating Saris*, 141–64.

# Bibliography

"Accommodation for Indian Dancer." *Canberra Times*, May 14, 1947, 3.
"Afghan Cameleers in Australia." *Australian Stories*, September 3, 2009. Accessed July 7, 2017. www.australia.gov.au/about-australia/australian-story/afghan-cameleers.
Ahmad, Aziz. *Studies in Islamic Culture in the Indian Environment*. Oxford, UK: Clarendon Press, 1964.
Ahmed, Y. Rafeek. "India's Membership of the Commonwealth: Nehru's Role." *The Indian Journal of Political Science* 52, no. 1 (1991): 43–53.
Allen, Margaret. "'A Fine Type of Hindoo' Meets 'the Australian Type': British Indians in Australia and Diverse Masculinities." In *Transnational Ties: Australian Lives in the World*, edited by Desley Deacon, Penny Russell, and Angela Woollacott, 41–58. Canberra: ANU E-Press, 2008.
Allen, Margaret. "'I Am a British Subject': Indians in Australia Claiming Their Rights, 1880–1940." *History Australia* (2018). doi:10.1080/14490854.2018.1485505.
Allen, Margaret. "Identifying Sher Mohamad: 'A Good Citizen'." In *Empire Calling: Administering Colonial Spaces in India and Australasia*, edited by Ralph Crane, C. Vijayasree, and Anna Johnston, 103–19. New Delhi: Oxford University Press, 2013.
Allen, Margaret. "'Innocents Abroad' and 'Prohibited Immigrants': Australians in India and Indians in Australia 1890–1910." In *Connected Worlds: History in Transnational Perspective*, edited by Ann Curthoys and Marilyn Lake, 111–24. Canberra: ANU E-Press, 2005.
Allen, Margaret. "Observing Australia as the 'Member of an Alien and Conquered Race'." In *Reading Down Under: Australian Literary Studies Reader*, edited by A. Sarwal and R. Sarwal, 560–70. New Delhi: SSS Publications, 2009a.
Allen, Margaret. "Otim Singh in White Australia." In *Something Rich and Strange: Sea Changes, Beaches and the Littoral in the Antipodes*, edited by Susan Hosking, Rick Hosking, Rebecca Pannell, and Nena Bierbaum, 195–212. Adelaide: Wakefield Press, 2009b.
Allen, Margaret. "Shadow Letters and the Karnana Letter: Indians Negotiate the White Australia Policy, 1901–1921." *Life Writing* 8, no. 2 (2011): 187–202.

# Bibliography

Allen, Matthew Harp. "Rewriting the Script for South Indian Dance." *The Drama Review* 41 (1997): 63–100.

Anandhi, S. "Representing Devadasis: 'Dasigal Mosavalai' as a Radical Text." *Economic and Political Weekly* 26, no. 11–12 (1991): 739–46.

Anderson, W. K., and S. D. Damle. *The Brotherhood of Saffron: The Rashtriya Swayamasevak Sangh and Hindu Revivalism*. New Delhi: Vistaar Publications, 1987.

Anoop, Maratt Mythili, and Varun Gulati, eds. *Scripting Dance in Contemporary India*. Lanham, MD: Lexington Books, 2016.

Artlover Madras, "Ananda Shivaram: India's Cultural Ambassador – White Australia Applauds *Rukmangada*." *Indian Express*, June 6, 1949, 3.

Arudra. "The Renaming of an Old Dance: A Whodunit Tale of Mystery." *Sruti* 27–28 (December 1986–January 1987): 30–31.

Ashley, Wayne. "Recodings: Ritual, Theatre, and Political Display in Kerala State, South India." PhD diss., New York University, 1993.

Au, Susan, and Jim Rutter. *Ballet and Modern Dance*. London: Thames & Hudson, 2012.

Aurobindo, Sri. *The Secret of the Veda*. Vol. 10. Pondicherry: Sri Aurobindo Ashram, 1971.

"Australian *Kathakali* Artiste Dead." *The Indian Express*, July 2, 1979.

Ayyappapanicker, K. *Kathakali: The Art of the Non-worldly*. Bombay: Marg Publications, 1993.

Bakhle, Janaki. "Country First? Vinayak Damodar Savarkar (1883–1966) and the Writing of Essentials of Hindutva." *Public Culture* 22, no. 1 (2010): 149–86.

Bakhle, Janaki. *Two Men and Music: Nationalism in the Making of an Indian Classical Tradition*. New York: Oxford University Press, 2005.

Banerjee, Sumanta. "'Hindutva': Ideology and Social Psychology." *Economic and Political Weekly* 26, no. 3 (1991): 97–101.

Banerjee, Utpal K. *Tagore's Mystique of Dance*. New Delhi: Niyogi Books, 2014.

Bapat, Guru Rao. *Re-scribing Tradition: Modernisation of South Indian Dance Drama*. Shimla: IIAS, 2012.

Basu, Tapan, Pradip Datta, Sambuddha Sen, Sumit Sarkar, and Tanika Sarkar. *Khaki Shorts, Saffron Flags: A Critique of the Hindu Right*. New Delhi: Orient Longman, 1993.

Bateson, Gregory. "Play and Paradigm." In *Play and Anthropological Perspectives*, edited by Michael A. Salter, 7–16. West Point: Leisure, 1977.

Bayly, Christopher. "India and Australia: Distant Connections." Keynote Address at the Australian Historical Association Conference, Adelaide, July 9, 2012. Accessed May 4, 2014. www.theaha.org.au/wp-content/uploads/2015/08/Bayley-2012_India-and-Australia.pdf.

Bayly, Susan. "Hindu Kingship and the Origin of Community: Religion, State and Society in Kerala, 1750–1850." *Modern Asian Studies* 18, no. 2 (1984): 177–213.

Beaver, Moya. "Interview with Michelle Potter." National Library of Australia Oral History Collection, October 13, 1994. Accessed May 4, 2014. www.nla.gov.au/amad/nla.oh-vn513088/0-1891~0-2080.

Bennett, Bruce, Santosh K. Sareen, Susan Cowan, and Asha Kanwar, eds. *Of Sadhus and Spinners: Australian Encounters with India*. New Delhi: HarperCollins, 2009.

Bilimoria, Purushottama. "Indian Dance." In *Currency Companion to Music and Dance in Australia*, edited by John Whiteoak and Aline Scott-Maxwell, 330–31. Sydney: Currency Press, 2003.

Bilimoria, Purushottama. "Of Dance & Theory: History of Indian Dance in Australia, from Lightfoot-Shivaram to Chandrabhanu." Paper Presented at Melbourne University South Asian Students Group, Melbourne, October 6, 2013. Accessed January 29, 2014. www.academia.edu/4766690/Of_Dance_and_Theory_History_of_Indian_Dance_in_Australia_from_Lightfoot-Shivaram_to_Chandrabhanu.

Bilimoria, Purushottama. "Speaking of the Hindu Diaspora in Australia." *Journal of Hindu-Christian Studies* 11 (1998): 11–19.

Bilimoria, Purushottama. "The Spiritual Transformation of Indian Dance in Australia – From Lightfoot to Aboriginal Corroboree." Paper Presented at the Conference on the Study of Religions of India: "Confounding and Contesting Religious and Cultural Boundaries," Knoxville, September 11–14, 2008.

Bilimoria, Purushottama. "Traditions and Transition in South Asian Performing Arts in Multicultural Australia." In *Culture, Difference and the Arts*, edited by Sneja Gunew and Fazal Rizvi, 108–29. Sydney: Allen and Unwin, 1994.

Bilimoria, Purushottama, Jayant Bapat, and Philip Hughes, eds. *The Indian Diaspora: Hindus and Sikhs in Australia*. New Delhi: D. K. Printworld, 2015.

Bose, Mandakranta. "The Evolution of Classical Indian Dance Literature: A History of Sanskritic Tradition." PhD diss., Oxford University, 1989.

Brissenden, Alan, and Keith Glennon. 2010. *Australia Dances: Creating Australian Dance, 1945–1965*. Kent Town, SA: Wakefield Press.

Brockington, J. *The Sacred Thread: Hinduism in Its Continuity and Diversity*. Edinburgh: Edinburgh University Press, 1996.

Broinowski, Alison. *About Face: Asian Accounts of Australia*. Melbourne: Scribe, 2003.

Broinowski, Alison. *The Yellow Lady: Australian Impressions of Asia*. Melbourne: Oxford University Press, 1996.

Card, Amanda. "History in Motion." PhD thesis, University of Sydney, 1999.

Cass, Joan. *The Dance: A Handbook for the Appreciation of the Choreographic Experience*. Jefferson, NC: McFarland, 2004.

Chaki-Sircar, Manjusri, and Parbati K. Sircar. "Indian Dance: Classical Unity and Regional Variation." In *India: Cultural Patterns and Process*, edited by Allen G. Noble and Ashok K. Dutt, 147–64. Boulder, CO: Westview, 1982.

Chakravorty, Pallabi. *Bells of Change: Kathak Dance, Women and Modernity in India*. Seagull Books, 2008. Calcutta.

Chakravorty, Pallabi. "From Interculturalism to Historicism: Reflections on Classical Indian Dance." *Dance Research Journal* 32, no. 2 (2000–2001): 108–19.

Champakalakshmi, R. *Religion, Tradition, and Ideology: Pre-colonial South India*. New Delhi: Oxford University Press, 2011.

Chandra, Suresh. *Encyclopaedia of Hindu Gods and Goddesses*. New Delhi: Sarup & Sons, 1998.

Chatterjea, Ananya. "Contestations: Constructing a Historical Narrative for Odissi." In *Rethinking Dance History: A Reader*, edited by Alexandra Carter, 143–56. New York: Routledge, 2013.

## Bibliography

Chatterjea, Ananya. "Dance Research in India: A Brief Report." *Dance Research Journal* 28, no. 1 (1996): 118–23.

Chatterjea, Ananya. "In Search of a Secular in Contemporary Indian Dance: A Continuing Journey." *Dance Research Journal* 36, no. 2 (2004): 102–16.

Chatterjee, Partha. *Nationalist Thought and the Colonial World*. London: Zed Books, 1986.

Chauhan, Viveka. *The Journey from Sadir to Bharatanatyam*. New Delhi: PSBT, 2015. Accessed March 5, 2018. www.youtube.com/watch?v=mD3RhhdaVTw.

Chelliah, Shobhana L. "Linguistics Asserting Nationhood Through Personal Name Choice: The Case of the *Meithei* of Northeast India." *Anthropological Linguistics* 47, no. 2 (2005): 169–216.

Coomaraswamy, A. K. *History of Indian and Indonesian Art*. London: Edward Goldston, 1927.

Coomaraswamy, A. K. *The Dance of Shiva*. New York: The Noonday Press, 1975.

Coorlawala, Uttara Asha. "Ruth St. Denis and India's Dance Renaissance." *Dance Chronicle* 15, no. 2 (1992): 123–52.

Coorlawala, Uttara Asha. "The Classical Traditions of *Odissi* and *Manipuri – Odissi: Indian Classical Dance Art* by Sunil Kothari; *Dances of Manipur: The Classical Tradition* by Saryu Doshi." Review. *Dance Chronicle* 16, no. 2 (1993): 269–76.

Craine, Debra, and Judith Mackrell. *The Oxford Dictionary of Dance*. Melbourne: Oxford University Press, 2010.

"Dancer Refused Room; Slept in Theatre." *Barrier Miner*, May 13, 1947, 2.

"Dancers' Art Delights." *Examiner*, April 13, 1950, 5.

"Dances of India: Colour and Poetry at University." *The Western Australian*, January 12, 1950, 6.

Dandré, Victor. *Anna Pavlova: In Art & Life*. New York: Arno Press, 1979.

Darwin, John. *Unfinished Empire: The Global Expansion of Britain*. London: Penguin Books, 2012.

Davis, Alexander E. "'A Shared History?' Postcolonial Identity and India-Australia Relations, 1947–1954." *Pacific Affairs* 88, no. 4 (2015): 849–69.

Davis, Richard S. "Introduction." In *Religions of India in Practice*, edited by David S. Lopez, Jr., 3–52. Princeton, NJ: Princeton University Press, 1995.

De Lepervanche, Marie M. *Indians in a White Australia*. Sydney: Allen and Unwin, 1984.

De Lepervanche, Marie M. "The (Silent) Voices of Indian Colies: Early Indian Workers in the Australian Colonies." In *Bridging Imaginations: South Asian Diaspora in Australia*, edited by Amit Sarwal, 58–84. New Delhi: Readworthy Publications, 2013.

De Triana, Rita Vega. *Antonio Triana and the Spanish Dance: A Personal Recollection*. London: Routledge, 2016.

Deshpande, Satish. "From Development to Globalization: Shifts in Ideological Paradigms of Nation and Economy in the Third World." In *Meanings of Globalization: Indian and French Perspectives*, edited by R. Melkote, 98–114. New Delhi: Sterling Publishers, 2001.

Desmond, Jane. "Dancing out the Difference: Cultural Imperialism and Ruth St. Denis's *Radha* of 1906." In *Moving History, Dancing Cultures. A Dance*

*History Reader*, edited by Ann Dils and Ann Cooper Albright, 256–70. Wesleyan: Wesleyan University Press, 2001.

Devi, Ragini. *Dance Dialects of India*. New Delhi: Motilal Banarsidass, 1990.

Doniger, Wendy, and Martha C. Nussbaum, eds. *Pluralism and Democracy in India: Debating the Hindu Right*. New Delhi: Oxford University Press, 2015.

Earnshaw, John. "Lang, John (1816–1864)." In *Australian Dictionary of Biography*. Canberra: National Centre of Biography, Australian National University, 1974. Accessed July 7, 2017. http://adb.anu.edu.au/biography/lang-john-3985/text6301.

Erdman, Joan. "Dance Discourses: Rethinking the History of the 'Oriental Dance'." In *Moving Words: Re-writing Dance*, edited by Gay Morris, 288–305. New York: Routledge, 1996.

Erdman, Joan. "Performance as Translation: Uday Shankar in the West." *Drama Review* 31, no. 1 (1987): 64–88.

Feuerstein, G., S. Kak, and D. Frawley. *In Search of the Cradle of Civilisation*. Wheaton, IL: Quest Books, 1995.

"First Woman Dancer from India Reaches Perth." *The West Australian*, January 7, 1950, 13.

Fischer-Lichte, Erika. *Dionysus Resurrected: Performances of Euripides' the Bacchae in a Globalizing World*. Hoboken: John Wiley & Sons, 2013.

Flood, Gavin D. *An Introduction to Hinduism*. Cambridge, UK: Cambridge University Press, 1996.

Fowler, Jeaneane D. *Hinduism: Beliefs and Practices*. East Sussex, UK: Sussex Academic Press, 1997.

"Friendly Indian Likes Us." *Sun Women's Magazine*, April 9, 1947.

Frost, Mark R. "Imperial Citizenship or Else: Liberal Ideals and the India Unmaking of Empire, 1890–1919." *The Journal of Imperial and Commonwealth History* 46, no. 5 (2018): 845–73.

Frykenberg, R. E. "The Emergence of Modem 'Hinduism' as a Concept and as an Institution: A Reappraisal with Special Reference to South India." In *Hinduism Reconsidered*, edited by Giinther D. Sontheimer and Hermann Kulke, 29–49. New Delhi: Manohar, 1989.

Gandhi, M. K. *To the Women: Gandhi Series*, edited by A. T. Hingorani. 3rd ed. Vol. 2. Karachi: Hingorani, 1946.

Gandhi, M. K. "Why I Am a Hindu." *Young India*, October 20, 1927. Accessed February 27, 2019. www.mkgandhi.org/truthisgod/22hindu.htm.

Gandhi, Rajmohan. *Modern South India: A History from the 17th Century to Our Times*. New Delhi: Aleph, 2018.

Ghosh, Partha S. *BJP and the Evolution of Hindu Nationalism: From Periphery to Centre*. New Delhi: Manohar, 2000.

Gibson, Josie. "Dancer's Dream Lives on." *Monash Magazine* 3 (Autumn–Winter 1999). Accessed April 9, 2013. www.monash.edu.au/pubs/monmag/issue3-99/item-05.html.

Goldsworthy, David. *Losing the Blanket: Australia and the End of Britain's Empire*. Melbourne: Melbourne University Press, 2002.

Gopal, Ram and Serozh Dadachanji. *Indian Dancing*. London: Phoenix House, 1951.

## Bibliography

Gopal, Ram. *Rhythm in the Heavens: An Autobiography*. London: Secker and Warburg, 1957.

Gould, William. *Hindu Nationalism and the Language of Politics in Late Colonial India*. Cambridge, UK: Cambridge University Press, 2004.

Grau, Andrée. "Dancing Bodies, Spaces/Places and the Senses: A Cross-cultural Investigation." *Journal of Dance & Somatic Practices* 3, nos. 1–2 (2011): 5–24.

Grierson, George A. "Bhakti-Marga." In *Encyclopaedia of Religion and Ethics*, edited by James Hastings, 539–51. New York: T. and T. Clark, 1940.

Griffin, Marion Mahoney. *The Magic of America*. Chicago: Art Institute of Chicago, 2007.

Guillebaud, Christine. "Music and Politics in Kerala: Hindu Nationalists Versus Marxists." In *The Cultural Entrenchment of Hindutva: Local Mediations and Forms of Convergence*, edited by D. Berti, N. Jaoul, and P. Kanungo, 29–63. New York: Routledge, 2011.

Habermas, J. *The Structural Transformation of the Public Sphere: An Inquiry into a Category of Bourgeois Society*. Cambridge, MA: MIT Press, 1991.

Hall, Fernau. "The Contribution of Indian Dance to British Culture." Paper Presented at the Academy of Indian Dance Seminar, Commonwealth Institute, London, June 29–30, 1982. Accessed April 16, 2013. www.vads.ac.uk/large.php?uid=47970.

Hall, Stuart. *Representation – Cultural Representations and Signifying Practices*. London: Sage Publications, 1997.

Hanna, Judith Lynne. *Dance, Sex, and Gender: Signs of Identity, Dominance, Defiance, and Desire*. Chicago: University of Chicago Press, 1988.

"Hindu Dance Artist: Symbolism and Beauty." *The Age*, April 29, 1947.

"Hindu Dancer Astounds with Muscle Control." *Advocate*, April 2, 1950.

"His English Is 'Very Bad' but His Dancing Is Good." *Sunday Times*, January 8, 1950, 8.

Horosko, Marian. *Martha Graham: The Evolution of Her Dance Theory and Training*. Gainesville, FL: University Press of Florida, 2002.

Hosking, Rick, and Amit Sarwal, eds. *Wanderings in India: Australian Perceptions*. Clayton: Monash University Press, 2012.

Hubel, Teresa. "The High Cost of Dancing: When the Indian Women's Movement Went After the Devadasis." In *Intercultural Communication and Creative Practice: Music, Dance, and Women's Cultural Identity*, edited by Laura Lengel, 121–40. Westport, CT: Praeger, 2005.

Hutton, Geoffrey. "Toward a Theatre; New Plays and Big Names Coming." *The Argus*, May 3, 1947, 17.

Inden, Ronald. *Imagining India*. Oxford, UK: Blackwell, 1992.

"Indian Dancer: Entrancing Display by Shivaram." *The West Australian*, February 16, 1948, 10.

"Indian Dancer Impressive." *The Argus*, April 29, 1947, 11.

"Indian Dancer Pleases Big Devonport Audience." *The Advocate*, April 19, 1950, 13.

"Indian Dances by Master." *Courier-Mail*, August 15, 1947, 7.

Jackson, A. V. Williams. "The Persian Dominions in Northern India Down to the Time of Alexander's Invasion." In *Ancient India*, edited by E. J. Rapson, 319–34. Cambridge, UK: Cambridge University Press, 1922.
Jain, Jyotindra. "India's Republic Day Parade, Restoring Identities, Constructing the Nation." In *India's Popular Culture: Iconic Spaces and Fluid Images*, edited by Jyotindra Jain, 60–75. Mumbai: Marg Publications, 2002.
Jeffrey, Robin. *The Decline of Nayar Dominance: Society and Politics in Travancore, 1847–1908*. London: Sussex University Press, 1976.
Jones, William. "The Four Yugs and Ten Avatars of the Hindoos." In *The Missionary Register*, 266–71. London: L. B. Seeley, 1820.
Joshi, Sashi, and Bhagavan Josh. *Struggle for Hegemony in India 1920–47*. 3 vols. New Delhi: Sage Publications, 1994.
Jost, Diana Brenscheidt. *Shiva Onstage: Uday Shankar's Company of Hindu Dancers and Musicians in Europe and the United States, 1931–38*. Berlin: LIT Verlag, 2011.
Katrak, Ketu H. *Contemporary Indian Dance: New Creative Choreography in India and the Diaspora*. Hampshire: Palgrave Macmillan, 2011.
Kersenboom-Story, Saskia C. *Nityasumangali: Devadasi Tradition in South India*. New Delhi: Motilal Banarsidass, 1987.
Khatun, Samia. *Australianama: The South Asian Odyssey in Australia*. New York: Oxford University Press, 2018.
Khokar, Mohan. *His Dance, His Life: A Portrait of Uday Shankar*. New Delhi: Himalayan Books, 1983.
Khokar, Mohan. *Traditions of Indian Classical Dance*. New Delhi: Clarion Books, 1979.
King, Anthony. "Spaces of Culture, Spaces of Knowledge." In *Culture, Globalization and the World System: Contemporary Conditions for the Representation of Identity*, edited by Anthony King, 1–39. Minneapolis: University of Minnesota Press, 1997.
King, Richard. "Orientalism and the Modern Myth of 'Hinduism'." *NUMEN* 46, no. 2 (1999): 146–85.
Klostermaier, Klaus K. *A Survey of Hinduism*. 3rd ed. New York: SUNY Press, 2007.
Kothari, Sunil. "Australian Diary: Part 2 – Interview with Kathakali and Mohiniattam Dancer Tara Rajkumar." *Narthaki.com*, August 17, 2009. Accessed March 4, 2019. www.narthaki.com/info/gtsk/gtsk9.html.
Kothari, Sunil, ed. *Bharata Natyam*. Mumbai: Marg Publications, 2007.
Kothari, Sunil. "New Directions in Indian Dance: An Overview 1980–2006." *Ausdance*, July 18, 2008. Accessed September 3, 2017. http://ausdance.org.au/articles/details/new-directions-in-indian-dance.
Kumar, Anu. "Meet Sujata and Asoka, the Indo-German Dancers Who Charmed Hollywood in the 1950s." *Scroll*, August 21, 2016. Accessed April 4, 2019. https://scroll.in/reel/814533/meet-sujata-and-asoka-the-indo-german-dancers-who-charmed-hollywood-in-the-1950s.
Lakhia, Kumudini. "Innovations in Kathak." In *New Directions in Indian Dance*, edited by Sunil Kothari, 60–69. Mumbai: Marg Publications, 2003.
Lawson, Valerie. "The First Australian Ballet." *Dance Australia Magazine*, March 1998.

Lightfoot, Mary Louise. "A Few Stories of Shivaram by His Australian Impresario." Typed Notes. Louise Lightfoot Collection, Music Archive of Monash University, 1947a. Accessed October 15, 2013.

Lightfoot, Mary Louise. "Explanation of Items by Miss Lightfoot's Hindu Dance Group." Louise Lightfoot Collection, Music Archive of Monash University, 1947b. Accessed October 15, 2013.

Lightfoot, Mary Louise. "International Appeal of the Ballet." *The Hindu*, February 11, 1940.

Lightfoot, Mary Louise. *Lightfoot Dancing: An Australian Indian Affair*. New York: Amazon Digital Services, 2015.

Lightfoot, Mary Louise. "Lightfoot, Louise." In *Dictionary of Sydney*. Sydney: State Library New South Wales, 2008. Accessed January 29, 2014. https://dictionary ofsydney.org/entry/lightfoot_louise.

Lightfoot, Mary Louise. "Two Thousand Years of Rhythm." *The Argus*, July 31, 1946, 16.

Lightfoot, Mary Louise, and Marian Quarterly. "Lightfoot, Louisa Mary (1902–1979)." In *Australian Dictionary of Biography*. Melbourne: Melbourne University Press, 2005. Accessed June 17, 2012. http://adb.anu.edu.au/biography/lightfoot-louisa-mary-13046.

Lille, Dawn. *Equipoise: The Life and Work of Alfredo Corvino*. New York: Dance Movement Press, 2010.

Lipner, Julius. *Life and Thought of a Revolutionary*. New Delhi: Oxford University Press, 1999.

Lipner, Julius. "On 'Hindutva' and 'Hindu-Catholic,' with a Moral for Our Times." *Hindu-Christian Studies Bulletin* 5, no. 1 (1992): 1–8.

Lochtefeld, James G. *The Illustrated Encyclopedia of Hinduism: A-M*. New York: The Rosen Publishing Group, 2002.

Lorenzen, David N. "Who Invented Hinduism?" *Comparative Studies in Society and History* 41, no. 4 (1999): 630–59.

Maclean, Kama. "Examinations, Access, and Inequity Within the Empire: Britain, Australia and India, 1890–1910." *Postcolonial Studies* 18, no. 2 (2015): 115–32.

Maclean, Kama. "India in Australia: A Recent History of a Very Long Engagement." In *Wanderings in India: Australian Perceptions*, edited by Rick Hosking and Amit Sarwal, 20–35. Clayton: Monash University Press, 2012.

"Malayalam." *The Age*, March 3, 1950.

"Many Offer Lodgings for Indian." *Advocate*, May 14, 1947.

Medcalf, Rory. "John Lang, Our Forgotten Indian Envoy." *The Spectator Australia*, March 31, 2010. Accessed July 7, 2017. https://web.archive.org/web/20100515040332/www.spectator.co.uk/australia/5880088/john-lang-our-forgotten-indian-envoy.thtml.

Meduri, Avanthi. "Bharatha Natyam: What Are You?" *Asian Theatre Journal* 5, no. 1 (1988): 1–22.

Meduri, Avanthi. "Labels, Histories, Politics: Indian/South Asian Dance on the Global Stage." *Dance Research* 26, no. 2 (2008a): 223–43.

Meduri, Avanthi. "The Transfiguration of Indian/Asian Dance in the United Kingdom: Contemporary 'Bharatanatyam' in Global Contexts." *Asian Theatre Journal* 25, no. 2 (2008b): 298–328.

Megarrity, Lyndon. "Regional Goodwill, Sensibly Priced: Commonwealth Policies Towards Colombo Plan Scholars and Private Overseas Students, 1945–72." *Australian Historical Studies* 38, no. 129 (2007): 88–105.
"Melbourne: Intercolonial Exhibition of Australasia 1866–67." Intercolonial and International Exhibitions, State Library of Victoria, June 30, 2017. Accessed July 7, 2017. http://guides.slv.vic.gov.au/interexhib/1866to67.
Menon, T. Madhava, ed. *A Handbook of Kerala*. 2 vols. Thiruvanthapuram, India: International School of Dravidian Linguistics, 2002.
Mill, James. *The History of British India*. 3 vols. London: Baldwin, Cradock and Joy, 1817.
Miller, Barbara Stoller. *Exploring India's Sacred Art: Selected Writings of Stella Kramrisch*. Philadelphia: University of Pennsylvania Press, 1983.
Minerva. "Theatre Royal Begins New Page in Its History Tonight." Music and Drama. *The Mercury*, March 31, 1950, 22.
Mishra, Vijay. *Devotional Poetics and the Indian Sublime*. New York: SUNY Press, 1998.
Monier-Williams, Monier. *Hinduism*. London: SPCK, 1894.
Munsi, Urmimala Sarkar. "Boundaries and Beyond: Problems of Nomenclature in Indian Dance History." In *Dance Transcending Borders*, edited by Urmimala Sarkar Munsi, 78–98. New Delhi: Tulika Books, 2008.
Nag, Kalidas, and Debajyoti Burman, eds. *The English Works of Raja Rammohun Roy*. Calcutta, India: Sadharan Brahmo Samaj, 1947.
Nandy, Ashis. "The Demonic and the Seductive in Religious Nationalism: Vinayak Damodar Savarkar and the Rites of Exorcism in Secularizing South Asia." In *Heidelberg Papers in South Asian and Comparative Politics: Working Paper No. 44*, edited by Subrata K. Mitra, 1–10. Heidelberg: University of Heidelberg, 2009. Accessed February 15, 2019. https://core.ac.uk/download/pdf/32580976.pdf.
Narayan, Shovana. *The Sterling Book of Indian Classical Dances*. New Delhi: New Dawn Press, 2004.
"National Theatre Movement of Australia." *Flyer*, March 1947. Louise Lightfoot Collection, Music Archives of Monash University, Accessed October 15, 2013.
Nauriya, Anil. "The Savarkarist Syntax." *The Hindu*, September 18, 2014. Accessed February 15, 2019. www.thehindu.com/2004/09/18/stories/2004091803791000.htm.
"Need for a New Type of School Teacher." *The West Australian*, January 9, 1950, 8.
Nevile, Pran. "Echoes of a Lost Tradition." *India Today*, August 15, 1996. Accessed September 3, 2017. http://indiatoday.intoday.in/story/book-extract-of-pran-nevile-nautch-girls-of-india-dancers-singers-playmates/1/282160.html.
NLAdance. "Indian Dance in Australia." List. Canberra: National Library of Australia, January 1, 2010. Accessed January 29, 2014. http://trove.nla.gov.au/list?id=1230.
O'Flaherty, Wendy Doniger. *Hindu Myths*. Middlesex: Penguin Books, 1982.
Orsini, Francesca. *The Hindi Public Sphere*. New Delhi: Oxford University Press, 2002.
O'shea, Janet. *At Home in the World: Bharat Natyam on the Global Stage*. Middletown, CT: Wesleyan University Press, 2007.
O'shea, Janet. "At Home in the World? The Bharatanatyam Dancer as Transnational Interpreter." *The Drama Review* 47, no. 1 (2003): 176–86.

Page, David. *Prelude to Partition: The Indian Muslims and the Imperial System of Control, 1920–1932*. New Delhi: Oxford University Press, 1982.

Pandeya, Gayanacharya Avinash C. *The Art of Kathakali*. Allahabad: Kitabistan, 1961.

Panikkar, Chitra. "Patrons, Troupes, and Performers." In *Kathakali: The Art of the Non-worldly*, edited by D. Appukuttan Nair and K. Ayyappa Paniker. *Special Issue of Marg: A Magazine of the Arts* 44, no. 4 (1993): 31–44.

Panikkar, K. M. *A History of Kerala, 1498–1801*. Annamalainagar: Annamalai University, 1960.

Paranjape, Makarand. *Decolonization and Development: Hind Svaraj Revisioned*. New Delhi: Sage Publications, 1993.

Paranjape, Makarand, ed. *Swami Vivekananda: A Contemporary Reader*. New Delhi: Routledge, 2015.

Paranjape, Makarand, and Sukalyan Sengupta, eds. *The Cyclonic Swami: Vivekananda in the West*. New Delhi: Samvad India, 2005.

Parpola, Asko. *The Roots of Hinduism. The Early Aryans and the Indus Civilization*. New Delhi: Oxford University Press, 2015.

Pask, Edward H. *Ballet in Australia: The Second Act, 1940–80*. Melbourne: Oxford University Press, 1982.

Pask, Edward H. *Enter the Colonies Dancing: A History of Dance in Australia, 1835–1940*. Melbourne: Oxford University Press, 1979.

Pathak, Avijit. "BJP Has Insulted My Hinduism." *The Wire*, April 7, 2019. Accessed April 10, 2019. https://thewire.in/religion/bjp-has-insulted-my-hinduism.

Pati, George. "Kerala." In *Brill's Encyclopedia of Hinduism: Regions, Pilgrimage, and Deities*, edited by Knut A. Jacobsen, 221–32. Vol. 1. Leiden: E. J. Brill, 2009.

Pattabhiraman, N. "The Trinity of Bharatanatyam: Bala, Rukmini Devi and Kamala." *Sruti* 48 (1988): 23–24.

Peterson, Indira Viswanathan, and Davesh Soneji, eds. *Performing Pasts: Reinventing the Arts in Modern South India*. New Delhi: Oxford University Press, 2008.

Potter, Michelle. "Ballet." In *Currency Companion to Music and Dance in Australia*, edited by John Whiteoak and Aline Scott-Maxwell, 70–77. Sydney: Currency Press, 2003.

Prabhavananda, Swami, and Frederick Manchester. *The Spiritual Heritage of India*. Madras: Sri Ramakrishna Mission, 1981.

Prashad, Vijay. *The Karma of Brown Folk*. Minneapolis: University of Minnesota Press, 2000.

Pratt, Mary Louise. "Arts of the Contact Zone." *Profession* 91 (1991): 33–40. Accessed May 15, 2014. www.nieuweleescultuur.ugent.be/files/meer_lezen2_pratt.pdf.

Prentiss, Karen Pechilis. *The Embodiment of Bhakti*. Cary: Oxford University Press, 2000.

Purie, R. D. "Dance Forms." Book Review. *India Today*, September 15, 1979. Accessed September 4, 2017. http://indiatoday.intoday.in/story/book-review-traditions-of-indian-classical-dance-by-mohan-khokar/1/427832.html.

Purkayastha, Prarthana. "Dancing Otherness: Nationalism, Transnationalism, and the Work of Uday Shankar." *Dance Research Journal* 44, no. 1 (2012): 69–92.

Qureshi, Regula. "Whose Music? Sources and Contexts in Indic Musicology." In *Comparative Musicology and the Anthropology of Music*, edited by Bruno Nettl and Philip Bohlman, 152–68. Chicago: University of Chicago Press, 1991.
Raghavan, M. D. *Folk Plays and Dances of Kerala*. Trichur, India: The Rama Varma Archaeological Society, 1947.
Rahman, Sukanya. *Dancing in the Family*. New Delhi: HarperCollins, 2002.
Rai, A. *Hindi Nationalism*. New Delhi: Orient Longman, 2001.
Rajkowski, Pamela. *In the Tracks of the Camelmen: Outback Australia's Most Exotic Pioneers*. North Ryde, NSW: Angus and Robertson, 1987.
Rajkumar, Tara. "Fragile Gesture: Indian and Western Approaches to Theatricality." In *World Dance '96: New Dance from Old Cultures*, 35–38. Melbourne: The Green Mill Dance Project, 1996.
Ramachandran, D. P. *Empire's First Soldiers*. New Delhi: Lancer Publishers, 2008.
Ramnarayan, Gowri. "Rukmini Devi: A Quest for Beauty, a Profile." Part I. *Sruti* 8 (1984a): 17–29.
Ramnarayan, Gowri. "Rukmini Devi: Dancer and Reformer, a Profile." Part 2. *Sruti* 9 (1984b): 17–29.
Ramnarayan, Gowri. "Rukmini Devi: Restoration and Creation." *Sruti: Indian Classical Music and Dance Magazine* 10 (August 1984): 26–38.
Ram-Prasad, C. "Contemporary Political Hinduism." In *The Blackwell Companion to Hinduism*, edited by Gavin Flood, 526–50. Oxford, UK: Blackwell Publishing, 2003.
"Record Enrolments for Summer School." *The West Australian*, January 4, 1950, 7.
Robinson, Harlow. *The Last Impresario: The Life, Times, and Legacy of Sol Hurok*. New York: Viking, 1994.
Roe, Jill. *Beyond Belief: Theosophy in Australia, 1879–1939*. Sydney: New South Wales University Press, 1986.
Roy, Arundhati. *The God of Small Things*. New Delhi: IndiaInk, 1997.
Russell, Elizabeth. "Louise Lightfoot: Dancing from East to West." *Dance Australia Magazine*, no. 8, 1982, np.
Rutledge, Martha. "Inglis, James (1845–1908)." In *Australian Dictionary of Biography*. Canberra: National Centre of Biography, Australian National University, 1972. Accessed July 7, 2017. http://adb.anu.edu.au/biography/inglis-james-3834/text6087.
Sachau, Edward C., ed. and trans. *Alberuni's India*. 2 vols. London: Kegan Paul, Trench, Triibner & Co., 1914.
Sahai, Baldeo. *The Sterling Book of Essence of Indian Thought*. New Delhi: Sterling Publishers, 2010.
Sana, Rajkumar Somorjit. *The Chronology of Meetei Monarchs (From 1666 to 1850 CE)*. Imphal, India: Waikhom Ananda Meetei, 2010.
Sarkar, Sumit. *Beyond Nationalist Frames: Postmodernism, Hindu Fundamentalism, History*. Bloomington: Indiana University Press, 2002.
Sarwal, Amit. "'A Kangaroo and Bradman': Indian Journalists' Visit to Australia Under the Colombo Plan, 1950–1957." *Journalism Studies* (2018). doi:10.1080/1461670X.2018.1428907.
Sarwal, Amit. *Labels and Locations*. Newcastle upon Tyne, UK: Cambridge Scholars Publishing, 2015.

Sarwal, Amit, ed. and comp. *Louise Lightfoot in Search of India: An Australian Dancer's Experience*. Newcastle upon Tyne, UK: Cambridge Scholars Publishing, 2017.

Sarwal, Amit. *South Asian Diaspora Narratives: Roots and Routes*. Jaipur: Rawat Publications, 2016.

Sastry, K. A. Nilakanta. *A History of South India: From Prehistoric Times to the Fall of Vijayanagar*. New Delhi: Oxford University Press, 1975.

Savarkar, Vinayak Damodar. *Hindutva: Who Is a Hindu?* Bombay: Veer Savarkar Prakashan, 1923/1969.

Scott-Maxwell, Aline. "Asia and Pacific Links." In *Currency Companion to Music and Dance in Australia*, edited by John Whiteoak and Aline Scott-Maxwell, 52–56. Sydney: Currency Press, 2003.

Sen, Geeti. "Return of the Prodigy." Interview. *India Today*, December 15, 1976. Accessed July 7, 2017. http://indiatoday.intoday.in/story/i-was-very-much-impressed-and-inspired-by-kathakali-ragini-devi/1/436881.html.

Seymour, Alan. "Presenting Louise Lightfoot." *Western Mail*, February 12, 1948, 51.

Shah, Purnima. "State Patronage in India: Appropriation of the 'Regional' and 'National'." *Dance Chronicle* 25, no. 1 (2002): 125–41.

Sharma, Arvind. "On Hindu, Hindustān, Hinduism and Hindutva." *Numen* 49, no. 1 (2002): 1–36.

Sharma, Jyotirmaya. *Hindutva: Exploring the Idea of Hindu Nationalism*. New Delhi: HarperCollins Publishers India, 2015.

Shaw, Jean. "Currently Narrating 'Kathakali' in Montreal." *Montreal Star*, March 2, 1959.

"Shivaram." Round Town. *The Mail*, May 31, 1947, 1.

"Shivaram Here on December 9th." *Benalla Ensign*, December 9, 1949, 6.

"Shunned Because of His Colour." *Advocate*, May 13, 1947, 5.

Smith, Wilfred Cantwell. *Meaning and End of Religion*. New York: Macmillan, 1963.

Soneji, Davesh. *Unfinished Gestures: Devadasis, Memory, and Modernity in South India*. Chicago: University of Chicago Press, 2012.

Sorell, Walter. *Dance in Its Time*. New York: Columbia University Press, 1986.

Srinivas, M. N. *Social Change in Modern India*. New Delhi: Orient Longman, 1989.

Srinivasan, Amrit. "Reform and Revival: The Devadasi and Her Dance." *Economic and Political Weekly* 20, no. 44 (1985): 1869–76.

Srinivasan, Amrit. "Temple 'Prostitution' and Community Reform: An Examination of the Ethno Graphic, Historical and Textual Context of the Devadasi of Tamil Nadu, South India." PhD diss., Cambridge University, 1984.

Srinivasan, Priya. *Sweating Saris: Indian Dance as Transnational Labor*. Philadelphia: Temple University Press, 2011.

Sugirtharajah, Sharada. *Imagining Hinduism: A Postcolonial Perspective*. London: Routledge, 2003.

"Tale of a Peacock Tail Picture." *Sunday Times*, January 15, 1950, 8.

Tarabout, Gilles. "Malabar Gods, Nation-building and World Culture: On Perceptions of the Local and the Global." In *Globalizing India: Perspectives from*

*Below*, edited by Jackie Assayag and Chris Fuller, 185–210. London: Anthem Press, 2005.

Tavan, Gwenda. *The Long, Slow Death of White Australia*. Melbourne: Scribe, 2005.

"Temple Dancer Says Fiji an Indian's Paradise." *The Mail*, 4.

"Temple Dancing Runs in Family." *Australian Women's Weekly*, April 15, 1950, 21.

Terry, Walter. *Ted Shawn: The Father of Modern Dance*. New York: Dial Press, 1976.

Thapar, Romila. *Interpreting Early India*. New Delhi: Oxford University Press, 1993.

Thapar, Romila. "Some Appropriations of the Theory of Aryan Race Relating to the Beginnings of Indian History." In *Invoking the Past: The Uses of History in South Asia*, edited by Daud Ali, 15–35. New Delhi: Oxford University Press, 1999.

Thapar, Romila. "The Theory of Aryan Race and India: History and Politics." *Social Scientist* 24, no. 1–3 (1996): 3–29.

Tharoor, Shashi. *Why I Am a Hindu*. New Delhi: Aleph Book Company, 2018.

"The First Australian Ballet (1929–1950)." Trove, National Library of Australia, January 1, 2010. Accessed January 27, 2014. http://trove.nla.gov.au/people/671050.

"The Life of Melbourne." *The Argus*, September 30, 1947, 8.

"The Nautch Girl." *The Maitland Daily Mercury*, December 27, 1907, 4.

Thobani, Sitara. *Indian Classical Dance and the Making of Postcolonial National Identities: Dancing on Empire's Stage*. New York: Routledge, 2017.

"Three New Acts at Majestic: Indian Dancer in Bright Revue." *The Advertiser*, May 13, 1947, 6.

Turnbull, J., and P. Y. Navaretti, eds. *The Griffins in Australia and India: The Complete Works and Projects of Walter Burley Griffin and Marion Mahony Griffin*. Melbourne: Miegunyah Press, 1998.

Unnikrishnan, C. P. "Ananda Shivaram Bids Farewell to the Aesthetic World." *Narthaki.com*, December 2001. Accessed June 24, 2013. www.narthaki.com/info/profiles/profile9.html.

Venkataraman, Leela. "Ambassador of Indian Dance." *The Hindu*, October 24, 2003. Accessed April 4, 2019. www.thehindu.com/fr/2003/10/24/stories/2003102401720500.htm.

Venkataraman, Leela. *Indian Classical Dance: The Renaissance and Beyond*. New Delhi: Niyogi Books, 2015.

Venu, Gopal. *The Language of Kathakali: Notations of 874 Hand Gestures*. Trichur, Kerala: Natana Kairali, 2000.

Vertinsky, Patricia, and Aishwarya Ramachandran. "Uday Shankar and the Dartington Hall Trust: Patronage, Imperialism and the Indian Dean of Dance." *Sport in History* 38, no. 3 (2018): 289–306.

Vox. "He Is a Planet Now." Out Among the People. *The Advertiser*, June 11, 1947, 4.

Walker, David. *Anxious Nation*. St Lucia, QLD: University of Queensland Press, 1999.

Walker, David. *Experiencing Turbulence: Asia in the Australian Imaginary*. New Delhi: Readworthy, 2013.

Walker, David. "National Narratives: Australia in Asia." *Media History* 8, no. 1 (2002): 63–75.

Walker, David, and Agnieszka Sobocinska, eds. *Australia's Asia: From Yellow Peril to Asian Century*. Crawley: UWA Press, 2012.

Ward, Stuart. *Australia and the British Embrace: The Demise of the Imperial Ideal*. Melbourne: Melbourne University Press, 2001.

Watson, Anne, ed. *Beyond Architecture: Marion Mahony and Walter Burley Griffin – America, Australia, India*. Haymarket, NSW: Powerhouse Publishing, 1998.

Weidman, Amanda J. *Singing the Classical, Voicing the Modern: The Postcolonial Politics of Music in South India*. Durham: Duke University Press, 2006.

Westrip, Joyce P., and Peggy Holroyde. *Colonial Cousins: A Surprising History of Connections Between India and Australia*. Adelaide: Wakefield Press, 2010.

Whaling, Frank. *Understanding Hinduism*. London: Dunedin Academic Press, 2009.

White, Richard. *Inventing Australia: Images and Identity, 1688–1980*. Sydney: Allen and Unwin, 1981.

Wilkinson, J. "The Return of Shivaram." *Spotlight*, November 1949, 8.

Willard, Myra. *History of the White Australia Policy to 1920*. Melbourne: Melbourne University Press, 1923.

Wilson, H. H. *The Religious Sects of the Hindus*. London: Christian Literature Society for India, 1904.

Yarrow, Ralph. *Indian Theatre: Theatre of Origin, Theatre of Freedom*. Surrey: Curzon, 2001.

Young, Michael. *The Elmhirsts of Dartington*. Totnes: Dartington Hall Trust, 1996.

Younger, Paul. *Playing Host to the Deity: Festival Religion in the South Indian Tradition*. New Delhi: Oxford University Press, 2002.

Zarrilli, Phillip. *Kathakali Dance Drama: Where Gods and Demons Come to Play*. London: Routledge, 2000.

Zarrilli, Phillip. *The Kathakali Complex: Actor, Performance and Structure*. New Delhi: Abhinav Publications, 1984.

Zubrzycki, John. *Jadoowallahs, Jugglers and Jinns: A Magical History of India*. New Delhi: Pan Macmillan India, 2018.

Zubrzycki, John. *The Last Nizam: An Indian Prince in the Australian Outback*. Melbourne: Pan Macmillan, 2006.

Zvelebil, Kamil. *The Smile of Murugan: On Tamil Literature of South India*. Leiden: E. J. Brill, 1973.

# Index

Note: Numbers in *italic* indicate figures on the corresponding page.

Aborigines 1, 104
Acharya, Abhinaya Gupta 31
Adult Education Board 117
Ahmad, Aziz 16
Ainsworth, Bette 63
Ainsworth, Gwen 63
Alberuni (Al-Biruni) 17
All India Khadi and Swadeshi Exhibition *87*
Allen, Margaret 2, 7
Allen, Matthew Harp 28
Anandhi, S. 35
anti-colonialism 2, 23
Antill, John 63
Ardell, Anita 118
Arts Council of Australia 117
Arundale, George S. 39, 60, *61*
Arundale, Rukmini Devi 11n38, 36, *38*, 39–40, 42, 46, 59, 60, *61*, 67, *68*
Aryan invasion theory 13, 15–16, 25n8
Asan, Kumaran 52n104
Ashton, Julian 60
Asian Relations Conference (New Delhi) *48*
Asoka (Ernst Rubener) 71, 88
*Attakatha* 43
Aurobindo, Sri 15, 19
Australia: colonial 1–2; culture of 117, 126; Indian perceptions of 7; links with India 1–2; Shivaram's impressions of 106–9, 111
Ayyappapanicker, K. 43

Bai, Maharani Sethu Parabati 46
Bakhle, Janaki 23, 36
Balagopalam 127
ballet 4, 39, 56, 58, 89; *Coppelia* 61, 76n30; Indian 66–7, 104; *Indira Vijayam* 98–9; *Lake of Swans* 70; *Le Carnaval* 63; *Le Spectre de la Rose* 63; *Les Sylphides* 63, *64*; *Oriental Impressions* 60; *Petrouchka* 63, 76n36; *Roksanda* 63; *Scheherazade* 63; *Swan Lake* 70; *Walpurgis Night* 63, *64*
Bandopadhay, Sruti 127
Banerjee, Sumanta 23
Baroda Nautch Girls *33*; *see also nautch* girls
Bateson, Gregory 30
Bayly, Susan 18
Beatles, The 4
Beaver, Moya 63, 65–6, 71, 77n67, 117
Bergner, Ruth 117, 119
*bhagtans* 32
*Bhakti* movement 18, 31
Bhangra 126
Bharata 31, 49–50n19, 100
Bharatanatyam 7, 36, 39, 40, 41, *68*, 87, 94, 117; Lightfoot's interest in 71
Bharatanatyam revival movement 36, 39–40, 46, 67
Bharatiya Janata Party (BJP) 23, 24
*Bhartiya Shastriya Nritya* 8; *see also* Indian dance, classical
Bhaskar 126

## Index

*bhava* 31
*Blue God, The* 68–70, *69*
Bollywood 126
Bose, Netaji Subash Chandra 23
British Empire 1–2
Britten, Terry 4
Brockington, J. 15
Burlakov, Misha 56, 58, *59*, 61, *62*, 63, 68, 70, 75n18, 117; in Paris 65–6; recital with Lightfoot 68

Cass, Joan 31
Castelcrag Dancing School 58
Cevi, Bimbavati 127
Chakravorty, Pallavi 35
Chandrabhanu 119
Chandralekha *123*
Chandravarkar, Justice 34
Chhau 117
Chitrasena Ballet 127
Christianity, indigenous 23
Clarke, Bruce 4
colonialism 1, 13, 47
communalism 23, 24
communists 46, 52n101
contact zone 4
Coomaraswamy, A. K. 42
Coorlawala, Uttara Asha 83
*Coppelia* 61–3, *62*, 76n30
*Cora, the Temptress* (musical opera) 4
"Cosmic Dance of Shiva, The" 11n36
Council of Adult Education 117
Cree, Jessie 61
culture: Aryan 13, 15; Australian 117, 126; English 45; Hindu 8, 13, 21, 47, 93; Indian 3, 17, 36, 75n6, 84, 117, 126; Indus Valley 13, 15; of Kerala 18; Vedic 18

Dalits 21, 24
dance: ballet 4, 39, 56, 58, 89, 98–9; Eurhythmic 56; folk 58; modern 58; *see also* Hindu dance; Indian dance
*Dance Brutale* 59
*dasiattam* 39
Davis, Richard H. 17
De Lepervanche, Marie 2
Deakin University 8
decolonisation 7
Denishawn 11n36

Desborough, Walter 109, 118
Deshpande, Satish 47
Devadasi Abolition Bill 40
*devadasis* 3, 8, 32, 34–5, 36, 39, 40, 67, 69
Devan, P. K. 119
Devi, Ibetombi 126
Devi, Ragini (Esther Luella Sherman) 4, 11n38
Devi, Rukmini *see* Arundale, Rukmini Devi
Doss, Nunda Lall 7
Dravidians 15, 18
*Dying Swan, The* (ballet) 11n34

Ellappa 94
Elmhirst, Dorothy 36
Elmhirst, Leonard 36
Erdman, Jean 4, 11n40
Erdman, John 4
eroticism 3
Evans, Dorothy 63
Evans, Sylvia 63
exoticism 4

facial expressions 44, 48–9, *99*, 103
Feminist Club 58
Fhandi, Rahul 24
Finch, Peter 63
First Australian Ballet 58, 61–3, 63, 65, 70
Flamenco dance 32
fundamentalism, Hindu 23–4

*Gandharva 37*
Gandhi, Kasturba *20*
Gandhi, Mahatma 19, *20*, 23, 25, *48*; on *devadasis* 35
Gayatri, V. 127
*Golden Threshold, The* (musical opera) 4
Goldsworthy, David 2
Gopal, Ram (Bissano Ram Gopal) 49, 84, *85*, 86, 88–9
Gopi, Kalamandalam 47
Gopinath, Guru 46, 92
Gould, William 24
Graham, Martha 4, 11n39
Grierson, G. A. 18
Griffin, George *55*
Griffin, Marion Mahoney 54–6, *55*, 58

Griffin, Walter Burley 54–6, *55*, 75n6
*gurukulam* 46

Hall, Fernau 4
Hall, Stuart 28
Hamilton, Gordon *69*, 70
hand gestures 30, 31, 45
Hanna, Judith Lynne 28
*Heart of Russia* 60
Heinz, Bernard 63
*Hermit, The* 112
Hindu culture 8, 13, 21, 47, 93
Hindu dance 36, 117, 127; Andalucian style 32; Bharatanatyam 7, 36, 39, 40, 41, *68*, 71, 87, 94, 117; *bhava* 31; and the dance of Shiva 30, 42; *dasiattam* 39; and Flamenco 32; Gandharva *37*; and Hinduism 28–31; innovations in 31–2; in the international circuit 126; key techniques 31; Manipuri 41, 113, 117; Mohiniyattam 41, 52n87, 117; *mudras* 31, 45; and Nataraja 28, *29*, 30, 41–2; Odissi 41, 117; *rasas* 31; reform movement 35–6; revival of 36; in royal courts 32; *sadir* 36, 39, 40, 67; in temples 2, 4, 7, 32, 71; traditional 48; use of gods and goddesses in 41; *see also* Indian dance
Hindu Dance Group 9, 13, 84
Hindu fundamentalism 23–4
Hinduism 7, 8, 13–14; and the arts 28; competition with Muslims 21, 23; ethos of 24–5; Gandhi's approach to 19, 21; and Hindu dance 28–31; vs. Hindutva 24; history of 18; militant 21, 27n52; and Nataraja 42; parallels with Biblical theories 14–15; reform movement 19; Savarkar's approach to 23; sects 17; Vedic period 15; *see also* Hindu dance
Hindustan 17–18
Hindutva 8, 13, 16, 19, 21, 23, 27n52, 49; vs. Hinduism 24; soft 24
Hurok, Sol 4, 11n37
Hutton, Geoffrey 99

identity: cultural 23, 47, 83; ethnic 23; Hindu 23, 24, 41; Indian 16, 41; national 19, 41; political 23; religious 19

imperialism 1, 23
India: Australian perceptions of 7; under British rule 19, 34; history of 14–17; links with Australia 1–2; as space for plurality, peace and tradition 25
India Culture Centre 87, 114n33
Indian culture 3, 17, 36, 75n6, 84, 117, 126
Indian dance: in Australia 2, 126; ballet 2, 4, 66–7, 104; classical 4, 7, 8–9, 31, 32, 36, 39, 40, 41, 48, 71, 117, 127; use of costumes and masks 100–1; in Europe 3; facial expressions in 44, 48–9, *99*, 103; hand gestures in 30, 31, 45; influence on Western dancers 4; key dance forms 41; traditional makeup for 99–100, 115n80; traveling troupes 46; in United States 3; with white dancers 3, 13, 32; *see also* Hindu dance; Indian dancers; Kathakali
Indian Dance Company 66
Indian dancers: *bhagtans* 32; as cultural diplomats 8, 9; *devadasis* 3, 8, 32, 34–5, 36, 39, 40, 67, 69; Gond dancers 47; Hindu Dance Group 9, 13, 84; *kalavangtis* 32; *nagar badhus* 32; *nautch* girls 3, *3*, 5, 8, 32, *33*, 34–5, 40, 83
*Indian Harvest Dance* 118
Indian High Commission 105
*Indian Maid, The* (ballet) 4
Indian music: accompanying dance 44; influence of 4
Indian National Congress (INC) 19
Indian Nationalism Movement 46
Indian Society of Oriental Art 84
*Indian Wedding* 59
*Indira Vijayam* 98–9
*Indo-Jazz Suite* 118
*Indra Vijayam* 113
Indrani 126
Indu settlements 2
Intercolonial Exhibition of Australasia 2
International Centre for Kathakali 47
Inyoka, Nyota 65
Iyer, E. Krishna 36
Iyer, Ulloor S. Parameswara 52n104

## 146  Index

Jacison, A.V. Williams 16
Jagat Singh II (Maharana) 5
Jan, Guahar 34
Jeffrey, Robin 18
Jinnah, Mohamad Ali 23, 27n52
Jones, William 14

Kalakshetra Dance Academy 67, 127
Kalamandalam 47
Kalashetra institute 39
*kalavangtis* 32
*Kamadeva* 112
Kathak 117
Kathakali: addition of chorus 101; in Australia 9, 13, 117; characteristics of 44–5; costumes and masks 99–100; decline in patronage for 45–6; differing agendas of 48; features of 44; as Indian classical dance 41; international promotion of 47–9; Lightfoot and Shivaram's adaptation of 101–2; Lightfoot's interest in 8, 67, 70–1; Lightfoot's promotion of 7, 9, 13, 73–5; Lightfoot's study of 78–9, 88, 90; modernisation of 46–7; *mudras* in 45; origins of 8, 18, 42–3, 77n60; representation of emotions in 44–5; revival of 46–47; Shivaram's performance of 47, 49, 81–3; in *Temple Dreaming* 124–6; traditional makeup for 99–100, 115n80; training for 43; Westernized form 84
Kerala 18, 43, 45, 67; categories of plays in 43–4
Kerala art 48
Kerala Communists 46
Kerala Kalamandalam 9, 47, 73, 81, 86, 127
Khan, Khan Abdul Ghaffar *48*
Khokar, Mohan 40
*King Rugmangadan* 113
Kothari, Sunil 30–1, 32, 36, 122, *123*
Kramrisch, Stella 84, 120
Krisanova, Nina 65
*Krishna and Radha* 60
Krishnamurti, Yamini *120*, 127
*Krishnanattam* 43
Kuchipudi 117
Kulkarni, Sreenivas 71, 91
Kurup, Gugu Kunchu 46

La Meri (La Marie) 4, 11n41, 36, 84, 88
*Lake of Swans* 70
Lakshmanan, Krishnaveni 127
Lang, John 1
Lawson, Valerie 62–3
*Le Carnaval* 63
*Le Spectre de la Rose* 63
*Les Sylphides* 63, *64*
Lightfoot, Lal 119–20
Lightfoot, Louise (Louisa Mary): as architect 54–6; archives at Monash University 120–3; in Bombay 88; choreographing *Petrouchka* 63; collaboration with Indian artists 7–8, 13; collaboration with Shivaram 4, 8, 9, 48, 75, 79–80, 83–4, 86–91, 93–113, 126; commended by Indian Government Trade Commisioner 117; dancing with Burlakov 56, 58; desire to bring Shivaram to Australia 82–3; family and background 54–6; in Fiji 111; involvement with Indian dance 8–9; journal entries and notes 12n53; as Kathakali's Australian mother 73–5, 120; in Kerala 70–1; at Kerala Kalamanadalam 78–9; later years 119; in Madras 86–7; meeting Uday Shankar 66–7; in Paris 65–6; photographs *55*, *59*, *62*, *72*, *73*, *87*, *96*, *112*, *120*, *121*, *122*; promotion of Indian dance 117; with Ram Gopal 88–9; return to India 70; in San Francisco 119; staging *Coppelia* 61–3; studying Bharatanatyam 94; studying Indian dance 42, 67–8; taking Indian dance to Australia 93–113; as teacher 65, 89, 90, 92; tour to Ceylon (Sri Lanka) 91–2; watching Pavlova 56; working with Shivaram 79–80
Lightfoot, Mary Louise 12n53, 58, 59, 63, 65, 67, 70, 95, 106, 111, 119, *123*
Lightfoot-Burlakov school/studio 8, 58, 60–1, 63, 68

Macledan, Kama 2
Madhavan 67, 113n6
Madras, Artlover 97–8

Madras United Artist Corporation (MUAC) 93
*Mahabharata* 79
Maharaj, Birju 127
Mahomed, Sher 7
Maling, Roy 63
Manipuri 41, 113, 117
Mansingh, Sonal 127
Martin, Frank J. 105
Martin, Pat 117
Masked Dancers of Bengal 127
Maya, Neena 71, 94, 95
McDonnell, Barbara 70
McIntyre, Colin *69*
Meduri, Avanthi 39–40
Megarrity, Lyndon 2
Menaka, Madame 36
Menon, Mahakavi Vallathol Narayana 46, 73, *81*
Mill, James 14
Minoutochka, Bertha 61
Mohini, Retna 84
Mohiniyattam 41, 52n87, 117
Monash University 119, 120–1, *123*; Music Archives 7, 120, 123, 124
Monier-Williams, M. 18
*Moorish Maid, A* (musical opera) 4
Morel, Paula 36
*mudras* 31, 45
Mukund Raja 46, 81
Munro, Charlie 4
Murlakov, Mischa 4
music: Australian 4; jazz 4; rock 4; *See also* Indian music
musical operas 4
Muslim League 23
Muslims: activists 24; competition with Hinduism 21, 23
mythology 30, 49n10

*nagar badhus* 32
Nair, Govindan 47
Nandikeshwara 31
Nandy, Ashis 23
Narayan, Shovana 30
Nataraja 28, *29*, 30, 41–2
nationalism: Hindu 24, 25, 49; Indian 23, 40, 41, 45, 46, 47, 90
Natya Sudha Dance Company 125–6
*Nautch, The* 11n35

*nautch* girls 3, *3*, 5, 8, 32, *33*, 34–5, 40, 83
Nayar Service Society (Nair Service Society) 45, 52n97
Nehru, Pandit Jawaharlal 23, 47–8, *48*, 52–3n107
Nevile, Pran 34–5
Nordi, Cleo 39

O'Connor, John 104
Odissi 41, 117
*Oriental Impressions 57*, 60
orientalism 47

Page, David 21
Pandeya, Gayanacharya Avinash C. 30, 43, 46, 100
Panicker (Pannikar), Gopala 80–1, *80*, 111
Panicker, Chathunni 47
Panigrahi, Sanjukta 127
Panikkar, Chitra 46
Paranjpye, Raghunath Purushottam 94, 97
Pathak, Avijit 24
Pattabhiraman, N. 39
Pavlova, Anna 4, 11n34, 36, 39, 56, *57*, 60, *60*
*Peacock Dance* 101, 104, *104*, 113, *118*
Peterson, Indira Viswanathan 40
*Petrouchka* (*Petrushka*) 63, 76n36
postcolonialism 40
Pratt, Mary Louise 4
prejudice 9, 104–7
Punjabi settlements 2

racial prejudice 9, 104–7
*Radha 6*, 11n35
Ragini 36
*Rajah of Shivapore, The* (musical opera) 4
Rajkumar, Tara 121–6, *123*, *125*, 127n17
*Ramanattam* 43
Ramgopal 71
Randell, Ronnie 63
*Ras Leela 110*, 112
*rasas* 31
Rashtriya Swayamsevak Sangh (RSS) 23

Ray, Jyotikana 127
Reddy, S. Muthulakshmi 35
Revid, Sonia 58
Robson, Ian C. 72
*Roksanda* 63
Roy, Arundhati 101
Roy, Raja Rammohan 19
Rubener, Ernst (Asoka) 71, 88
*Runga Pooja* 112
Russell, Betty 117

*sadir* 36, 39, 40, 67
Sahitya Natak Akademi 41
Salear, Mrs Minnie 109
San Francisco University 119
Sangeet Natak Akademi 41
Sanskrit language 15, 18, 19
Sarabhai, Mallika 127
Saraswati, Vishnudevananda 119, 127n10
Sauer, Carl 60
Savarkar, Vinayak Damodar 21, *22*, 23, 27n52
*Scheherazade* 63
See India Foundation 119
Sergieff, Ivan 58, 66
Seymour, Alan 71, 82, 107
Shankar, Rajendra 87–8
Shankar, Uday *3*, 8–9, 36, *37*, 39, 49, *60*, 66, 84, 87, 90, 111, 114n33
Shankara, Adi 18
Sharma, Arvind 14
Shawn, Ted (Edwin Myers Shawn) 4, 11n36, 107
Sherman, Esther Luella (Ragini Devi) 4, 11n38
Sheth, Daksha 127
Shiv Sena 23
Shivaram, Ananda: in Ceylon (Sri Lanka) 71, 91–2; background and family 80; collaboration with Lightfoot 4, 8, 9, 48, 75, 79–80, 83–4, 86–91, 93–113, 126; as cultural ambassador 117–18; in Fiji 111; impressions of Australia 106–9, 111; in Kerala 90; as Lord Indra 99; Man-Lion pose *106*; in *Peacock Dance 104*, *118*; performing in Australia 96–7, 98–105, *98*, *102*, 112–13, 117–18; performing

Kathakali 47, 49, 81–3; in Perth 107, *108*; photographs *79*, *80*, *87*, *96*, *99*, *102*, *104*, *106*, *108*, *110*, *112*, *118*; in *Ras Leela 110*; in San Francisco 119; in Tasmania 107, 109; teaching Kathakali 118, 119 ; training 81–82
Sievers, Gertrude 56
Singh, Otim 7
Singh, Rajkumar Priyagopal 94, 126
Sinha, Guru Banamali 127
Sinha, Kamini Kumar 92
Smith, Wilfred Cantwell 19
Social Purity Associations 34–5
socio-religious reform 45
Soneji, Davesh 40
Song and Dance Theatre 127
Srinivasan, Amrit 34, 40
St. Denis, Ruth 4, *6*, 11n35
*Stars and Garters* 104
stereotypes 4
Subramanyam (Subramaniam), K. 71, 92–3
Sugirtharajah, Sharada 14, 19, 28
Suguna Vilasa Sabha 36
*Sultan's Choice, The* (ballet) 4
*Swan Lake* 70

Tagore, Rabindranath 36
Tamil Nadu 45
Tarabout, Gilles 46
*Temple Dreaming* 121–6, *123*, *125*
Teolar, Mrs K. C. 105, 109
Thapar, Romila 14, 16
Tharoor, Shashi 24
Theosophical Society 58
theosophy 39, 58, 51n56
Thobani, Sitara 3, 32, 41
Thomas, Mrs Wilfred 109
Tilakavati 126
*Twilights, The* 4
two-nation theory 23, 27n52

University of Western Australia 107
Unnikrishnan, C. P. 101
Upadhyay, Brahmabandhav 23
Uthram Thirunal Majaraja 45

Vaishnavism 19
Vallathol, Sri Mahakavi 11n38, 36, 46, 47, 52n104, 84, 86, 119

van Buitenen, J.A.B. 17
*Varnashrama* 21
Vedic Aryans 13
Vega de Triana, Rita 31–2
Venkatraman, Leela 84, 86
Vishwa Hindu Parishad (VHP) 23
Vivekananda, Swami 19, 25
Vyajayanthimala 127

Walker, David 2
Wallace, Jimmy 104
*Walpurgis Night* 63, *64*
Ward, Stuart 2

Welch, Leona 117
White Australia Policy (WAP) 2
Whitelock, Trafford 63
Wigman, Mary 58
Williamson, J.C. 61, 89
Wilson, H. H. 18

Yarrow, Ralph 4
*Yogi, The* 11n35
Young Bengal Group 19

Zarrilli, Phillip 45
Zoroastrianism 16

# Taylor & Francis eBooks

www.taylorfrancis.com

A single destination for eBooks from Taylor & Francis with increased functionality and an improved user experience to meet the needs of our customers.

90,000+ eBooks of award-winning academic content in Humanities, Social Science, Science, Technology, Engineering, and Medical written by a global network of editors and authors.

## TAYLOR & FRANCIS EBOOKS OFFERS:

- A streamlined experience for our library customers
- A single point of discovery for all of our eBook content
- Improved search and discovery of content at both book and chapter level

## REQUEST A FREE TRIAL
support@taylorfrancis.com

For Product Safety Concerns and Information please contact our EU representative  GPSR@taylorandfrancis.com
Taylor & Francis Verlag GmbH, Kaufingerstraße 24, 80331 München, Germany

www.ingramcontent.com/pod-product-compliance
Lightning Source LLC
Chambersburg PA
CBHW051646230426
43669CB00013B/2468